The Aestheticienne

THE AESTHETICIENNE

Simple Theory and Practice

ANN HAGMAN SRN, Cert Ed, MPhys

in association with

William Arnould-Taylor MSc PhD

Fellow of The Royal Society of Medicine

Stanley Thornes (Publishers) Ltd

First edition published in 1981 by
Stanley Thornes (Publishers) Ltd
Old Station Drive
Leckhampton
CHELTENHAM GL53 0DN

Reprinted 1983 with minor corrections
Reprinted 1984
Reprinted 1987
Reprinted 1990

British Library Cataloguing in Publication Data

Hagman, Ann
    The aestheticienne.
    1. Beauty culture
    I. Title
    646.7′2   TT957

    ISBN 0–85950–308–9

Set in Garamond by Quadraset Limited, Radstock, Bath
Printed in Great Britain at The Bath Press, Avon

Contents

Part B Treatments

Part C   Salon Management

Foreword

It gives me much pleasure to write a foreword for a book which was specially commissioned for the International Therapy Examination Council but which will obviously fill the much greater need of an easily understandable textbook for general Aestheticienne education.

The author, Ann Hagman, is very well qualified to write such a book. As a State Registered Nurse of considerable experience she has a wide knowledge of people and their needs. To this experience is added that of being Principal of a private Beauty Therapy training school as well as running a successful clinic – a happy combination of theory and practice.

In wishing the book all the success which I am sure it will achieve I would commend it to all schools and colleges undertaking any aspect of Beautician/Aestheticienne training.

W E Arnould-Taylor
Chairman Examination Board
International Therapy Examination Council

Preface

It has been felt that a new book, written in simple terminology, would be of use to students of aesthetics, particularly if they are hoping to take the examination of the ITEC.

I would like to express my gratitude to: Mrs Beryl Elms, for her deciphering and subsequent typing of the manuscript; Miss Christine Long for her proof-reading; Mr W E Arnould-Taylor for his content reading, his professional help and encouragement; and above all my husband, Ronald Hagman, who has assisted and supported me during the time it has taken to write this book.

Ann Hagman
1981

PART A
Anatomy and Physiology

Today, everybody wants to look good and to feel good. The aestheticienne is someone who can help achieve this. Among the studies that she will learn are skin cleansing and facial massage, eyelash tinting and make-up, the use of electrical instruments upon the face, hair removal by waxing or electrolysis, manicure and pedicare and other treatments. It is apparent that she does not work very much upon the rest of the body. This is left to the Physical Therapist or Physiatrist.

The aestheticienne should have a clear understanding of elementary anatomy, that is the study of the structure of the body, and physiology, which is the study of the function of the various systems of the body, particularly ones which are most affected by her professional skills. But her primary concern is the skin. This is what her hands come in contact with. She will, however, work over the superficial muscles and peripheral nerves, she will stimulate the vascular system and advise on diet so as to aid digestion. All this will help to produce a more healthy skin.

The following chapters have been written for the student with little or no knowledge of the subject. The different systems have been simply described without overemphasising points that do not concern the aestheticienne.

A book will assist a student with her studies. It will not take the place of a tutor or her practical experience.

Chapter 1

Introduction

To make learning easier, the anatomy is divided into eight systems. In some textbooks this may be subdivided to make nine or ten systems. For the purpose of this book the skin is also treated as an individual subject.

No system should be viewed in total isolation as no one system can function on its own but relies on all the others.

MAJOR SYSTEMS

There are four major systems, so-called because they affect the whole of the body. They are the ones which are most affected by the aestheticienne. They are:

(1) the **skeletal** system;

(2) the **muscular** system;

(3) the **vascular** system;

(4) the **neurological** system.

Each will be discussed later in detail (see Chapters 3 – 6).

MINOR SYSTEMS

The other four systems are referred to as minor systems because they are not fully affected by the aestheticienne. However, they play a major role in the health and general condition of the whole body. We will now describe these briefly.

The Digestive System

This is responsible for taking food into the body. Food is digested and absorbed so that it can give sustenance to the rest of the body. This system also deals with the removal of unwanted matter. The aestheticienne will come into indirect contact with this system when she advises her client on diet.

The Respiratory System

This is the system whereby oxygen is taken into the lungs and thence into the blood stream, and where carbon dioxide is taken from the blood and exhaled out of the body. Occasionally an aestheticienne may be called upon to assist a patient with respiratory problems.

The Urinary and Genital Systems

These two systems have a number of common organs, but the aestheticienne will not have much contact with them. The urinary system generally helps to extract waste matter and unwanted salts – mostly sodium chloride, phosphates and sulphates – from the blood and so helps to keep it at its normal alkaline level. The genital system is responsible for reproduction.

The Endocrine System

This is a very complicated system and is not directly affected by an aestheticienne. The effects of this system are, however, of great importance in the aestheticienne's work. The ductless glands secrete their hormones directly into the blood stream. Their functions are all closely related and one balances another. If one is upset, the rest can become unbalanced and overproduce their hormones. A good example is when the adrenal gland puts out insufficient cortisone. The pituitary gland (hypophysis) will then stimulate the adrenal gland to work extra hard. The cortisone is produced, but as the adrenal gland also produces androgens, these are overproduced, thereby creating hypertrichosis.

As an aestheticienne works over a specific area of the body, she must remember that all eight systems may be affected by her work. No one system can work on its own.

SOME BASIC TERMINOLOGY

Before moving on to more detailed study of anatomy and physiology, the aestheticienne should first have an understanding of a little of the basic terminology:

Anatomy – the study of the structure of the body.

Physiology – the study of the functions of the various systems of the body.

Histology – the microscopic study of tissue.

Pathology – the study of the cause of a disease which involves changes in the structure and function of the body.

Morphology–concerned with the study of structure and form.

Natural anatomical position – the human body in an erect position, with the arms hanging loosely by the sides and the palms of the hands facing forward.

Anterior or **ventral view** – the front aspect of the body in the erect position.

Posterior or **dorsal view** – the rear aspect of the body in the erect position.

Median line – the middle of a structure; for example an imaginary line which runs through the centre of the body from the crown of the head to between the feet.

Medial – towards the midline of the body; for example the inner side of the arm.

Lateral – furthest away from the midline; for example the outer side of the arm.

Proximal – nearest to the heart or median line. Thus the thigh is the 'proximal' end of the leg.

Distal – furthest away from the heart or median line. The foot is at the 'distal' end of the leg.

Peripheral – the surface or outer edge. The nerves of the hand are part of the 'peripheral' nervous system.

Superficial – lying near the surface. The skin is superficial.

Deep – away from the surface. We can say that the femur lies 'deep' in the leg.

Symmetrical – used when parts of the body are similar. Two blue eyes of similar colour could be called 'symmetrical'.

Superior or **cephalic** – towards the head and upper part of the body.

Inferior – away from the head; for example the lower part of the body.

Supine – in the horizontal position, lying on the back.

Prone – in the horizontal position, lying face down.

Chapter 2

The Skin

THE LAYERS OF THE SKIN

For the aestheticienne the skin is the most important organ.

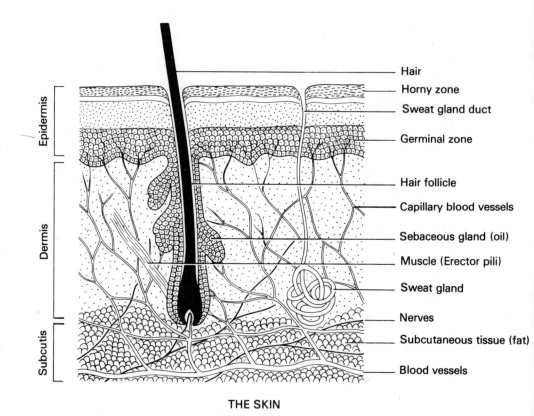

Epidermis
— Hair
— Horny zone
— Sweat gland duct
— Germinal zone

Dermis
— Hair follicle
— Capillary blood vessels
— Sebaceous gland (oil)
— Muscle (Erector pili)
— Sweat gland

Subcutis
— Nerves
— Subcutaneous tissue (fat)
— Blood vessels

THE SKIN

Dermatology is the study of the skin and is essential in making a correct diagnosis thus enabling the appropriate treatment to be given.

The skin consists of three layers:

(1) the **epidermis**;
(2) the **dermis**;
(3) the **subcutis**.

The Epidermis

The most superficial layer, it varies in thickness, being thickest on the soles of the feet and palms of the hands and very much thinner on the face. The eyelids are finer still. It contains no blood vessels or nerves.

Some text-books may give different names and subdivisions for the five layers.

The epidermis is divided into two zones:

(1)   the **horny** zone;

(2)   the **germinal** zone.

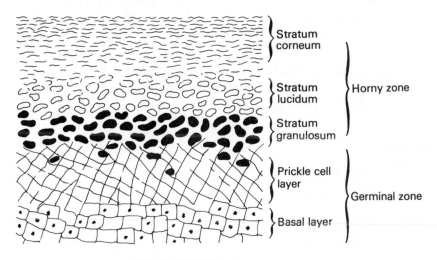

Stratum corneum

Stratum lucidum

Stratum granulosum

Horny zone

Prickle cell layer

Basal layer

Germinal zone

THE EPIDERMIS

The Horny Zone

The horny or upper zone is sub-divided into three layers:

The stratum corneum is the most superficial layer. It consists of thin keratinised cells. They have no nucleus or natural protective oils. If they are exposed to too much heat or sunlight or are roughly treated, they will become completely dehydrated and will become dry, flaky scales. The outer layer of dead cells are continually being shed.

The stratum lucidum consists of transparent cells, usually without nuclei, which permit light to pass through.

The stratum granulosum consists of distinctively shaped cells, containing a number of granules with some cells still having their nuclei. This layer links the living cells of the epidermis to the dead cells above.

The Germinal Zone

This zone is divided into two layers:

The prickle cell (spinosum) layer, so named because each cell is connected to the next by thin fibres giving them a prickly appearance. They are living cells containing a nucleus.

The basal (germinative or malphigian) layer. It is in this layer that the new epidermal cells are constantly being reproduced. These cells last about six weeks from reproduction before being discarded into the horny layer. It is in this layer that there are a number of cells called *melanocytes.* These cells produce a pigment called *melanin.* This gives the skin colour, determining whether one is fair skinned, brown or black. An absence of melanin produces totally white hair and pink eyes with poor vision, a condition known as *albinism.* Melanocytes react to ultraviolet radiation, whether emitted naturally from the sun or artificially from a lamp. By producing melanin, the skin is protecting itself from the penetrating ultraviolet rays. The darker one's skin, the more protection one has.

The Dermis

Sometimes called the *true skin,* the dermis is formed of tough, flexible connecting tissue. It contains:

Capillary Blood Vessels

A fine network of capillary blood vessels which supply oxygen and nutrients to the skin. Deoxygenated blood is carried away by a fine meshwork of veins to the larger vascular system and thence back to the lungs.

Lymphatic Vessels

Lymphatic vessels drain away waste products.

Sensory Nerve Endings

Sensory nerve endings carry impulses to the brain. Tactile nerves end in rounded pads, while the fine tracery nerve endings carry the stimuli of pain, heat, cold, etc.

Sweat (Sudorific) Glands

There are two kinds of sweat or sudorific glands, and they are found all over the body. The apocrine are found in greater numbers in the axillae and groin. Their functions are to help regulate body heat and eliminate waste materials. They often open into a hair follicle. When the body perspires, the sweat from these glands mixes with surface bacteria and causes body odour. The eccrine glands are found all over the body. They excrete mainly water with a little salt.

Sebaceous Glands

Sebaceous glands are also found all over the skin. They usually, but not always, open into hair follicles. They are found in great numbers on the scalp, face and sometimes the back. They secrete an oily substance called sebum which helps to keep the skin moist and the hair soft. Too much sebum gives the skin and hair a greasy appearance. Too little results in dry, brittle hair and dry skin.

If the pores become blocked, trapping the sebum and sweat, blackheads, whiteheads, spots and other conditions can arise.

Hair

Hair can be found over nearly all the body except on the palms of the hands, the soles of the feet and the lips. It varies in length, colour and texture in different areas of the same body and in different ethnic groups. The hair root lies beneath the skin and the shaft above it.

The Subcutis

Formed of loose connective tissue, the subcutis separates the dermis from the underlying muscle and permits the skin to move easily over it. An ample supply of blood and lymph vessels, nerve endings and fat cells are found here. The fat cells act as a storage depot and are thicker in women, giving them a more feminine, rounded appearance. The fat also helps reduce heat loss.

THE FUNCTIONS OF THE SKIN

The functions of the skin may be described as follows:

Protection

Through the fat cells of the subcutis, the skin protects the body against blows and falls. The horny layer acts as a barrier against bacteria and excess fluid. The germinal layer protects the body from harmful and ultraviolet light.

Sensation

Because the skin contains so many tactile nerve endings the brain can easily be made aware of the different stimuli of pain, cold, heat, etc. in any part of the body.

Heat Regulation

The skin helps to regulate the body temperature through the secretion of the sweat glands and constriction (contraction) or dilation (expansion) of the blood vessels in the dermis.

Excretion and Secretion

The skin excretes waste material through the sweat glands which also help control the fluid loss from the body. As already mentioned, the sebaceous glands secrete a substance called sebum which helps to keep the skin oily and supple. Sebum also assists in producing an acid mantle over the skin which is of great importance in limiting the activity of bacteria.

Absorption

The skin is able to absorb some oil or fat based substances, but not water.

DISORDERS OF THE SKIN

Below are some of the terms used in dermatology to describe various disorders of the skin:

Erythema – a general reddening of the skin.

Pigmentation – a variation in skin colour due to the amount of melanin deposits in the skin.

Lesion – a change in tissue formation.

Macule – a small area of abnormal colour.

Papule – a firm raised lesion up to a centimetre in size.

Nodule – a larger raised lesion.

Wheal – a slightly raised lesion, white at the centre, pale red at the edge, accompanied by itching.

Vesicle – a small blister containing fluid.

Bulla – a larger blister containing fluid.

Pustule – similar to a papule but containing pus.

Scale – a thin dry exfoliation from the surface of the skin.

Crust – a scab, which may contain dry serum, blood or pus.

Ulcer – an interruption of the continuity of the surface of the skin, having an inflamed base.

Wart – an elevation of the skin resulting from overproduction of prickle cells, caused by a virus.

Wen – a cyst resulting from the retention of sebum.

Vitiligo – areas of milky white skin surrounded by normal pigmentation. It is more noticeable in darker skin.

Cloasma – brown areas of skin caused by an increase of melanin. Often associated with pregnancy and advancing age, also certain chemicals.

Seborrhoea – an excessive production of sebum.

Comedones – commonly called blackheads. Formed by sebum trapped in the pores. The surface becomes hardened with oxidised keratin and turns black.

Closed comedones – plugs of sebum completely enclosed by skin.

Acne Vulgaris – one of the most common skin conditions. It can affect the face, neck, back or chest. This condition is most common at puberty, affecting both sexes. It may be caused by an increase of the sex hormones which can create conditions that allow the growth of bacteria on the skin. It starts as seborrhoea, then comedones and closed comedones will appear. Some of these will develop into pustules, which may rupture and spread infection. Treatment must be very carefully performed or severe scarring will result. Usually the earlier this condition appears, the longer it lasts.

Acne Rosacea – chronic congestion of the superficial blood vessels down the centre of the face. There may be broken veins complicated by papules. This condition can be exaggerated by anything causing vasodilation – heat, sunshine, spiced food, alcohol, cold. It particularly affects women of menopausal age. It has nothing to do with acne vulgaris.

Dermatitis – an inflammation of the skin characterised by erythema, itching and various skin lesions, such as papules and vesicules. It can affect both sexes, at any age in any climate. There are many causes:
Plants (tomato, daffodil, etc.)
Drugs (penicillin, antihistamine, etc.)

Clothing (certain dyes, wool, synthetic materials, metal zips, etc.)
Cosmetics (lipsticks and nail polish, perfume, some hair dyes, etc.)
Chemicals (detergents, petroleum and its by-products, etc.).

Eczema – similar to dermatitis but of unknown origin. The different types are:
Atopic (hereditary, relating to asthma, hay fever, urticaria)
Infantile
Childhood
Adult.

Boil – an acute inflammation of the subcutaneous layer of skin, gland or hair follicle caused by a staphylococcal infection producing suppuration.

Carbuncle – a deeper seated infection than a boil.

Urticaria – (also called **hives** and **nettle rash**). An allergy marked by the eruption of wheals with severe itching. It may appear on one part of the body and disappear, only to reappear elsewhere. It can be caused by certain food, drugs, insect bites, pollens.

Hyperidrosis – a disorder of the sweat glands causing increased sweating.

Abscess – a localised formation of pus usually requiring lancing (cutting open) by a doctor.

Skin Cancer – affects those areas of the body that are most often exposed to the sun. It may start as a pale lesion, a red patch or a coloured mole. If there is any *rapid* change in appearance – becoming larger, changing colour or becoming ulcerated – it *may* indicate skin cancer. It is not usually painful.

GLOSSARY

Connective tissue	Loosely connected cells forming a continuous sheet together with an intracellular substance (matrix) which supports and connects other tissues
Contagion	Where a specific disease is transferred either by direct or indirect contact with an infected person
Granules	Small grains
Infection	What occurs when part of the body is invaded by viruses or micro-organisms which multiply. This causes an inflammation

and possibly the formation of pus. It can be directly caused by an abrasion or injury but can also be transmitted by air, water, insects, food, human carriers and direct contact

Keratin   A fibrous protein which forms the chemical basis of hair, nails and horny tissue

Malpighian   Originally described by Marcello Malpighi

Nucleus   The vital body in a cell essential for its growth and reproduction

Self-infection   What occurs when infection is transmitted from one part of the body to another. This frequently occurs in cases of acne vulgaris

Septic foci   A local area of infection where pus is usually present, characterised by boils, carbuncles or abscesses

Chapter 3

The Skeletal System

THE SKELETON

The whole skeleton consists of 206 bones. They can be classified as **long** bones, **short** bones, **flat** bones, **irregular** bones and **sesamoid** bones.

Their function is to provide a framework for the rest of the body and to afford protection for vital organs. To assist in locomotion and stability, they act as points of attachment for tendons and muscles so that limbs can be moved at the point of articulation.

If bones were formed of solid masses, they would be too heavy for the rest of the body tissue to support. They consist of fibrous tissue to give them strength and rigidity, interspersed with minute cavities. The bone tissue consists of approximately 25% water, 30% organic matter and 45% minerals. These minerals are mainly calcium phosphate and traces of magnesium salts.

Bones are protected by a thin membrane known as the **periosteum**. This is richly supplied by blood vessels and nerves.

THE SKULL

The skull of an average adult weighs approximately 10 lb. It consists of 22 bones, some flat, some irregular, which fuse close together in early infancy to form an immovable casing. The only movable bone is the mandible.

The function of the skull is to protect the brain and give form to the face.

The Cranium

The eight bones forming the cranium are:

1 **frontal** bone   2 **temporal** bones

2 **parietal** bones   1 **sphenoid** bone

1 **occipital** bone   1 **ethmoid** bone

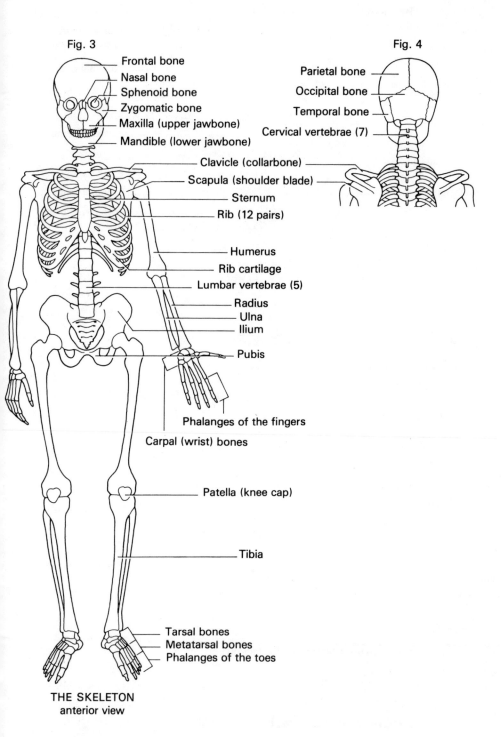

Fig. 3

Frontal bone
Nasal bone
Sphenoid bone
Zygomatic bone
Maxilla (upper jawbone)
Mandible (lower jawbone)

Clavicle (collarbone)
Scapula (shoulder blade)
Sternum
Rib (12 pairs)

Humerus
Rib cartilage
Lumbar vertebrae (5)
Radius
Ulna
Ilium
Pubis

Phalanges of the fingers

Carpal (wrist) bones

Patella (knee cap)

Tibia

Tarsal bones
Metatarsal bones
Phalanges of the toes

THE SKELETON
anterior view

Fig. 4

Parietal bone
Occipital bone
Temporal bone
Cervical vertebrae (7)

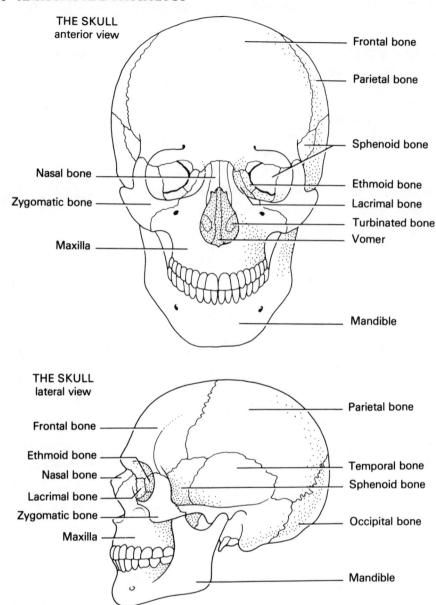

THE SKULL
anterior view

Frontal bone

Parietal bone

Sphenoid bone

Nasal bone

Ethmoid bone

Zygomatic bone

Lacrimal bone

Turbinated bone

Maxilla

Vomer

Mandible

THE SKULL
lateral view

Parietal bone

Frontal bone

Ethmoid bone

Nasal bone

Temporal bone

Lacrimal bone

Sphenoid bone

Zygomatic bone

Maxilla

Occipital bone

Mandible

Face Bones

The fourteen bones of the face are:

2 **maxillary** bones

1 **mandibular** bone

2 **zygomatic** bones (**malar**)

2 **nasal** bones

Internal Facial Bones

And the internal facial bones:

2 **palatine** bones ⑨

1 **vomer** bone

2 **lacrimal** bones

2 **inferior conchae** bones (**turbinated**)

Auditory Bones

Inside each ear are three small bones:

1 **stapes** bone (**stirrup**)

1 **incus** bone (**anvil**)

1 **malleus** bone (**hammer**)

Hyoid Bone

In front of the trachea is the:

Hyoid bone or **Adam's apple**

GLOSSARY

Bone sinus   An air cavity in the bone structure

Cancellous bone   A spongy bone formed by connecting bands of bone tissue interspersed with spaces filled with marrow

Compact bone   Harder and less porous bone, usually found surrounding cancellous bone

Osteo-   Pertaining to bone

Osteology   The study of bones

Sinusitis   An infection of the facial sinus

Chapter 4 The Muscular System

MUSCLES

There are over 640 named muscles in the body and many thousands of unnamed ones including many *erector pili* muscles which make our hair stand on end.

A muscle is a band of elastic (contractile) tissue bound together in bundles. A number of these contractile fibres are held together by a sheath. The ends of these sheaths are extended to form tendons by which the muscles are attached.

CROSS-SECTION
THROUGH MUSCLE

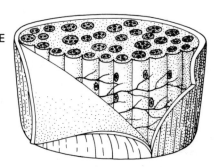

There are two types of muscles: **voluntary** muscles, which are usually under conscious control and can be moved at will, and **involuntary** muscles, over which we have no control. These include the muscles involved in respiration and digestion, and the heart.

HOW MUSCLES WORK

Muscles are moved as a result of a nervous stimulus which they receive from the brain via a motor nerve. When a muscle is working, it *contracts* by shortening its length and becoming fatter at the centre or belly.

MUSCLE CONTRACTING

MUSCLE RELAXING

Muscles usually work in pairs. The one that is working is known as the *prime mover* or *synergist*. The second muscle is holding it in check as a counter balance and is known as the *antagonist*. Even when muscles are at rest or relaxing, they are under slight tension and it is this tension that is called *muscular tone*.

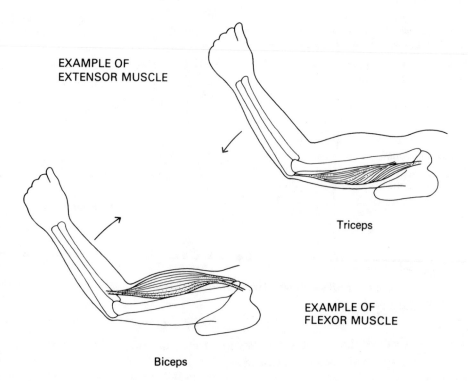

EXAMPLE OF
EXTENSOR MUSCLE

Triceps

EXAMPLE OF
FLEXOR MUSCLE

Biceps

In the case of the arm, when it is held out in front, the biceps muscle in the forearm becomes the *antagonist* and the triceps muscle becomes the *synergist* or *prime mover*. As it also extends the arm it has become known as an *extensor* muscle. When the arm is bent at the elbow, the biceps muscle becomes the *synergist*, but it also becomes a *flexor* muscle.

Muscles receive their food and oxygen from the arterial blood. This is converted into energy by chemical changes which break down glucose, glycogen and lipids (fats).

Waste products such as lactic acid and urea are excreted from the muscles into the venous systems. Some particles are too large for this system so they are collected by the lymphatic system.

The muscles of the face, neck and scalp lie just below the skin.

MAIN SCALP MUSCLES

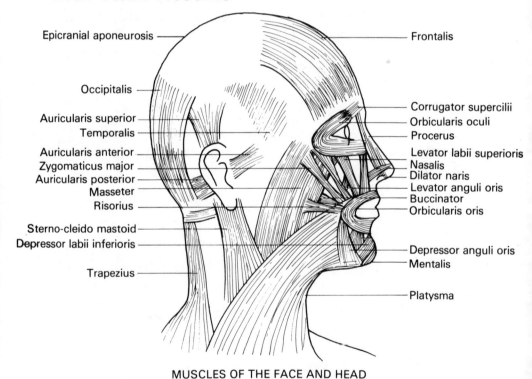

MUSCLES OF THE FACE AND HEAD

The main muscles of the scalp are:

Occipitalis – covers the base of the skull and occipital bone and draws the scalp backwards.

Frontalis – covers the frontal bone, raises the eyebrows and draws the scalp forward. It also causes lines on the forehead. It is sometimes called the *muscle of attention*.

Together these two muscles are known as the **occipitofrontalis.**

MAIN FACE MUSCLES

The main muscles of the face include:

Eyebrows and lids

Orbicularis Oculi – circular sphincters which surround the eyes and close them.

Levator palpebral – open and close the eyelids.

Corrugator supercilii – runs along the eyebrows and causes frown marks.

Nose

Procerus – covers the top of the nose and wrinkles it.

Nasalis – covers the tip of the nose and compresses it.

Depressor Septi – near the upper lip, elevates the side of the nose.

Dilator Naris, Posterior and Anterior – in the nasal cavity, they dilate the nostrils.

Mouth

Orbicularis Oris – a sphincter surrounding the mouth and closing the lips, known also as the *kissing muscle*.

Levator Labii, Superior – *above* the upper lip, it lifts the lips.

Depressor anguli oris – *under* the lower lip, it pulls the mouth down.

Levator anguli oris – above the upper lip, it lifts the corners of the mouth. It is also known as the *muscle of threat*.

Zygomaticus major – stretches from the zygomatic bone to the corners of the mouth. It lifts the corners of the mouth when laughing.

Mentalis – covers the tip of the chin, and is also known as the *muscle of disgust.*

Depressor labii inferioris – situated at the side of the mouth and chin, it pulls down the corners of the mouth. It is also known as the *muscle of sadness.*

Risorius – this muscle, which is at the side of the mouth, lifts the corners of the mouth when smiling.

Buccinator – also at the side of the mouth, compresses the cheeks and is known as the *whistling muscle.*

Mastication 3.

Temporalis – shaped like a shell, it runs down the side of the face from the temporal bone to the mandible. It helps to close the mouth.

Masseter – a broad muscle running from the zygomatic bone to the angle of the mandible. It helps to close the mouth when chewing.

Pterygoids, external and internal – these muscles run from the mandible to the spheroid and palatines bones. They move the mandible in all directions: up and down, side to side and from back to front.

Ears

These muscles are very rudimentary in humans.

Auricularis Anterior – in front of the ear, it draws the ear forward slightly.

Auricularis Superior – this muscle is above the ear and can raise the ear slightly.

Auricularis Posterior – behind the ear, it draws the ear back slightly.

MUSCLES OF THE NECK AND SHOULDERS

Platysma – runs up the throat and acts on the skin of the lower lip and neck.

Sterno-cleido Mastoids – run up the front of the neck from the sternum to the mastoid processes. If used separately, it turns the head from one side to the other. If used together, they flex the neck.

Trapezius – found at the back of the chest and neck. It braces and raises the shoulders and extends the neck.

Spinatus Erectae – extends the vertebral column.

GLOSSARY

Aponeurosis	A flat sheet of connective tissue which serves to attach muscles to bone or other tissue
Atrophy (dystrophy)	A reduction in the size of a muscle. A wasting process
Ligament	A band of strong fibrous connective tissue, connecting bones, cartilage or muscles
Muscle fascia	The sheath which covers and contains a muscle
Muscular fatigue	A reduction in the amount of work that a muscle can perform
Myology	The study of muscles
Rupture	A tearing of the fascia
Sprain	Injury to a ligament
Strain	Injury to a muscle
Tendon	Fibrous connective tissue which attaches muscles to bone or other tissue

Chapter 5 The Neurological System

DIVISIONS OF THE NEUROLOGICAL SYSTEM

The neurological system is the vehicle for transmitting messages between the brain and the other parts of the body.

It has three main divisions:

(1) the **central (cerebrospinal)** nervous system:
(2) the **autonomic (sympathetic** and **parasympathetic)** nervous system;
(3) the **peripheral** nervous system.

THE CENTRAL NERVOUS SYSTEM

The central nervous system consists of the *brain* and *spinal cord.*

The Brain

The brain is the most important part of the nervous system. It receives impulses and stores them in a retrieval system known as the memory.

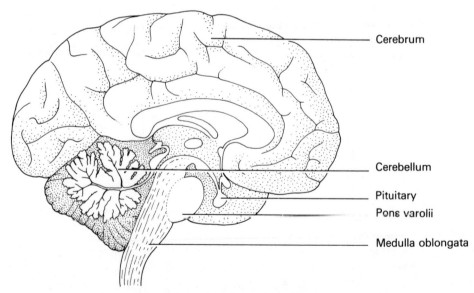

SECTION THROUGH THE BRAIN

It transmits impulses to all parts of the body in order to stimulate other organs to act. The brain is well protected, first by the scalp, hair and skin and then by the skull.

Inside the skull are three coverings called *meninges*. The outer one is called the *dura mater*. This is a tough fibrous membrane which helps to cushion the brain against the inside of the cranium. It has a deep fold in it which supports and separates the two parts of the cerebrum. It has another fold separating the cerebellum from the cerebrum. (It also encloses and protects the spinal cord.) The *arachnoid mater* is a delicate membrane which lies just under the dura mater. The *pia mater* is the inner covering. It closely folds into the convolutions of the surface of the brain and surrounds the spinal cord. For added protection, between the arachnoid mater and the pia mater there is a clear colourless fluid known as the *cerebrospinal fluid*.

The brain consists of three main parts:

(1) the **cerebrum**;
(2) the **cerebellum**;
(3) the **brain stem**.

The Cerebrum

The cerebrum, or large brain, is divided into two *hemispheres*. The surface is called the *cerebral cortex* and consists of nerve cells or grey matter. To increase the number of nerve cells it has indentations called *convolutions*. Separating them are deeper *fissures*. Underneath the cortex and filling the interior of each hemisphere lies a mass of *nerve fibres* or white matter.

The functions of the cerebrum are to interpret conscious sensations and transmit motor impulses that control voluntary muscular movements. It is also the centre of memory, reasoning and intelligence.

The Cerebellum

The cerebellum, or small brain, lies below and behind the cerebrum. Like the cerebrum it has an outer layer of grey matter enclosing an inner mass of white matter. Its functions are to control muscular coordination and maintain muscular tone. Because it receives impulses from the semicircular canals of the ear as well as the muscles, it also assists in balance and equilibrium.

The Brain Stem

The brain stem consists of:

(1) the **mid-brain**;

(2) the **pons varolii**;

(3) the **medulla oblongata.**

The *mid-brain* joins the two cerebral hemispheres to the *pons varolii* which acts as a bridge to the cerebellum. Together they convey impulses to and from the cerebrum and cerebellum. The *medulla oblongata* is a very important structure connecting the other parts of the brain to the spinal cord. Impulses from the right side of the body are transmitted via this 'telephone exchange' to the left side of the brain and vice versa. The *medulla oblongata* also contains a mass of grey matter known as the *vital centre* which controls the part of the autonomic nervous system responsible for respiration, the heart and blood vessels and certain gastric processes.

The Spinal Cord

The spinal cord is continuous with the *medulla oblongata* and extends downwards through the vertebral column, to the level of the first lumbar vertebra. It is surrounded by the *meninges* and *cerebrospinal fluid.* Given off from the spinal cord are thirty one pairs of *spinal nerves* corresponding to the segments of the vertebral column.

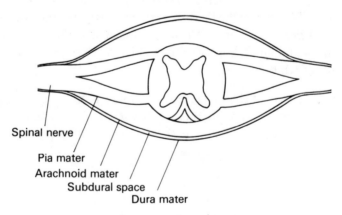

Spinal nerve

Pia mater
Arachnoid mater
Subdural space
Dura mater

SECTION OF THE SPINAL CORD

THE AUTONOMIC NERVOUS SYSTEM

The autonomic nervous system controls the body structures over which there is no conscious control. It regulates the *visceral functions* such as the cardiac muscles, digestion, respiration, urinary, genital and vascular muscles. It is also responsible for the *nervous reflex action*.

THE PERIPHERAL NERVOUS SYSTEM

The peripheral nervous system connects the central nervous system to all parts of the body. Nerves carrying impulses from the brain are known as *motor* or *efferent*. Nerves carrying impulses to the spinal cord and brain are known as *sensory* or *afferent*. Mixed nerves consist of both motor and sensory nerve fibres.

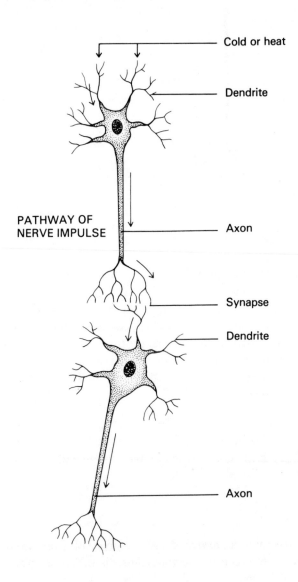

Cold or heat

Dendrite

PATHWAY OF NERVE IMPULSE

Axon

Synapse

Dendrite

Axon

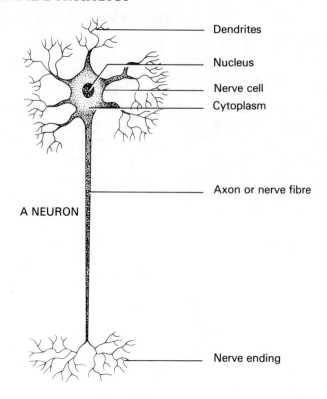

Dendrites

Nucleus

Nerve cell

Cytoplasm

Axon or nerve fibre

A NEURON

Nerve ending

Nerves

Nerves are formed by the joining of nerve cells called *neurons*. Each cell body contains a nucleus and is surrounded by a mass of *cytoplasm*. The small fibres that bring impulses to the cell body are called *dendrites*. The larger fibre which conducts impulses away from the cell body are called *axons*. In order for impulses to travel along a nerve they must go from the axon of one neuron to the dendrite of the next neuron and the place where the nerve endings of the axon and dendrite meet is called the *synapse*.

There are two types of *nerve fibres*: (1) *white* fibres which are surrounded by a sheath of myelin and are called *medullated fibres* and (2) *grey* fibres which have no myelin sheath and are called *non-medullated fibres*.

Cranial Nerves

Twelve pairs of *cranial nerves* are given off from the brain stem. It is these with which the aestheticienne is most concerned.

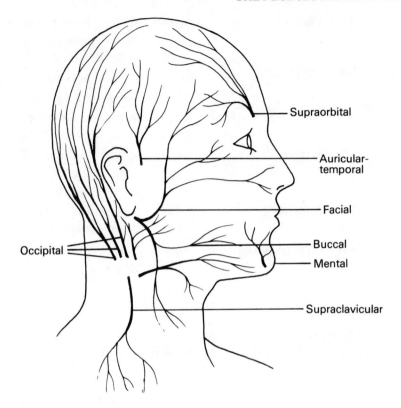

- Supraorbital
- Auricular-temporal
- Facial
- Buccal
- Mental
- Supraclavicular
- Occipital

NERVES OF THE FACE AND HEAD

The 12 pairs of cranial nerves are

	Name	Type	Function
(1)	Olfactory	sensory	sense of smell
(2)	Optic	sensory	sense of sight
(3)	Oculo motor	motor	supplies muscles which move the eyes
(4)	Trochlear	motor	supplies the superior oblique muscles of the eyes
(5)	Trigeminal	mixed	sensory fibres convey sense of taste, pain, heat and pressure to the tongue as well as the skin of the face. Motor fibres stimulate the muscles of mastication
(6)	Abducent	motor	stimulates the eyeball making it contract

(7)	Facial	mixed	sensory fibres to the tongue. Motor fibres govern muscles of facial expression
(8)	Auditory	sensory	sense of hearing affects equilibrium and balance
(9)	Glassopharyngeal	mixed	sensory to the tongue. Motor to the muscles of the pharynx
(10)	Vagus	mixed	sensory and motor fibres controls digestive and respiratory organs
(11)	Accessory	motor	controls trapezius and sterno-cleido-mastoid muscles
(12)	Hypoglossal	motor	controls movement of the tongue

Motor Points

Muscles are moved by contraction and their movements are caused by an electrical impulse sent by the brain via nerves. Every muscle in the

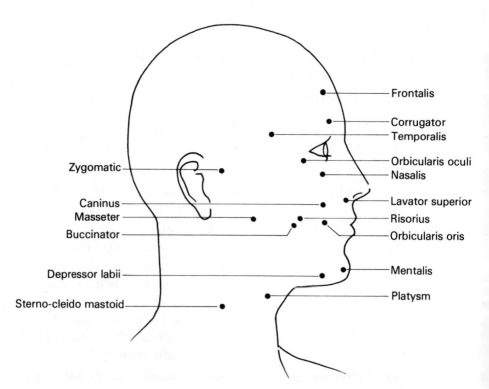

MOTOR POINTS OF THE FACE

body receives stimulation from one or more nerves, although the muscles of the face usually only have a single nerve supply. The greatest concentration of stimulation is usually where the nerve enters the deep surface of the muscle, often near the point of origin. This concentration is called the motor point.

GLOSSARY

Ganglion   A mass of nerve tissue lying outside the brain or spinal cord
Neuralgia   Severe pain along the course of a nerve
Neuritis   Inflammation of a nerve
Peripheral   Being near the surface of the body
Plexus   A group of intertwined nerves

Chapter 6

The Vascular System

The vascular system is comprised of the **blood circulatory system** and the **lymphatic system**.

THE BLOOD CIRCULATORY SYSTEM

The blood circulatory system basically consists of the **heart, arteries, veins** and **blood**.

The Heart

The heart weighs about nine ounces and is the organ which pumps blood around the body. It is divided into four chambers. The right and left side are separated by a solid muscular *septum.*

Venous blood enters the heart at the *right atrium (auricle),* from the lower part of the body by the *inferior vena cava* and from the upper part of the body by the *superior vena cava.* It passes into the *right ventricle.*

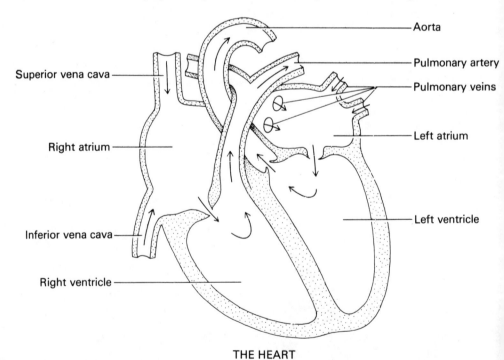

THE HEART

It leaves this chamber via the *pulmonary artery* and is taken to the lungs where carbon dioxide is taken out of the blood and oxygen is taken in.

Blood returns to the heart via the *pulmonary veins* to the *left atrium (auricle)* then into the *left ventricle*. It leaves the heart by the *aorta*, and then passes through a series of *arteries* to all parts of the body.

Arteries

Arteries are hollow elastic tubes which carry blood away from the heart. As they spread through the body and become smaller they are known as *arterioles* and finally the very small vessels called *capillaries*.

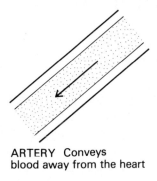

ARTERY Conveys
blood away from the heart

Veins

Veins are also hollow elastic tubes and carry blood towards the heart. They have *valves* which prevent the blood from flowing backwards.

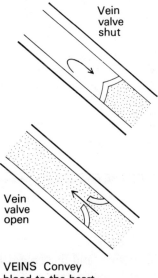

Vein
valve
shut

Vein
valve
open

VEINS Convey
blood to the heart

Blood

Blood is carried to the superficial structures of the head from the heart by the *aorta* which first divides into the *common carotid arteries* and then *external carotid artery*. This divides into arterial branches such as:

the **facial** artery;

the **maxillary** artery;

the **occipital** artery;

the **lateral nasal** artery;

the **posterior auricular** artery;

the **temporal** artery.

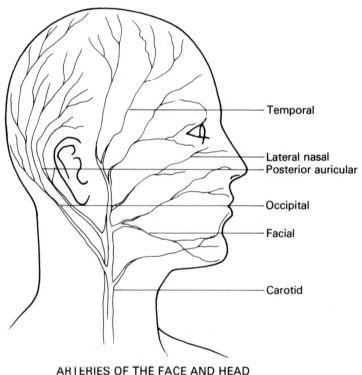

Temporal

Lateral nasal
Posterior auricular

Occipital

Facial

Carotid

ARTERIES OF THE FACE AND HEAD

These repeatedly divide and become smaller until they become capillaries all over the face and scalp.

Blood is collected from the superficial structures of the head in the capillaries and passes along branches of:

the **temporal** vein;

the **occipital** vein;

the **posterior auricular** vein;

the **maxillary** vein;

the **common facial** vein;

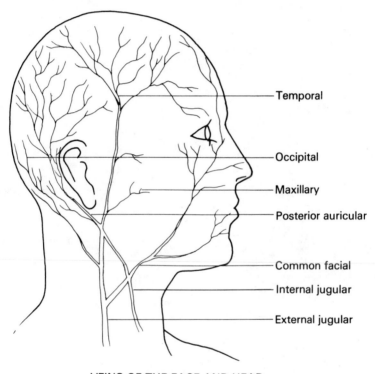

Temporal

Occipital

Maxillary

Posterior auricular

Common facial

Internal jugular

External jugular

VEINS OF THE FACE AND HEAD

to the **internal** and **external jugular** veins into the **brachiocephalic** vein and enters the heart via the **superior vena cava.**

There are about six litres of blood in the average adult. It consists of:

Plasma – a straw-coloured fluid which carries such substances as sugars, amino-acids, mineral salts, urea, etc.

Erythrocytes (red corpuscles) – biconcave discs containing a substance called haemoglobin which carries oxygen.

Leucocytes (white corpuscles) – larger than erythrocytes, they have an irregular shape and contain a nucleus. They help the body to combat infection by overpowering and ingesting bacteria.

Thrombocytes (platelets) – small cells which are essential to the body as they help to form clots with a substance known as fibrinogen.

THE LYMPHATIC SYSTEM

The lymphatic system consists of a series of blind-ended canals leading into lymph nodes and lymph.

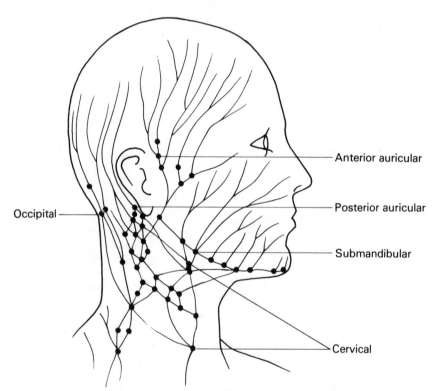

LYMPHATIC NODES AND VESSELS OF THE FACE AND HEAD

Lymph is usually a clear, colourless fluid containing proteins, salts, organic substances and water but no erythrocytes.

The lymph canals carry lymph drained from the capillaries and particles such as protein and carbon, too large to be carried in the venous system.

The lymph nodes which act as filters and help to prevent infection spreading above these points interrupting the canals. The main nodes draining the face are the *submandibular* near the jaw and the *anterior auricular nodes* in front of the ears. The main nodes of the body are the *axillary* in the armpits, the *epitrochlear* at the elbow, the *inguinals* in the groins and the *popliteal* at the knees.

The lymph canals empty into two large ducts: the *thoracic* which starts in the abdomen, and the *right lymphatic* duct near the *subclavicular node*.

They finally empty into the *left* and *right subclavian veins* where they join the jugular vein and so the lymph is returned to the blood stream from which it originally came.

GLOSSARY

Biconcave disc A disc having a spherical depression on both sides

Carbon dioxide (CO_2) A colourless gas containing carbon and oxygen, which is produced by combustion or decomposition. It is given off by the body in air exhaled from the lungs and is the final combustion product of food that has been used as energy by the body.

Fibrinogen A protein present in the blood plasma. When blood is exposed to a foreign substance, a new substance, *thrombin,* converts fibrinogen into a stringy mesh in which the thrombocytes become entangled and so form a clot.

Haemoglobin A chromo-protein of red colour that consists of an iron-containing pigment and a simple protein which has the ability to combine with oxygen and so transport it

Nucleus The vital body of a cell necessary for growth and reproduction

Septum A membranous wall dividing two cavities

Valve (venous) A flap of membrane which closes a vein after blood has pushed past it thus preventing the blood from flowing back the way it has travelled

Chapter 7

Hands, Feet and Nails

THE WRIST AND HAND

Bones

The wrist, or carpus, is composed of eight small irregular bones which interlock and are held together by ligaments. The movement between any two is small, but when they are all moved together there is great flexibility. The bones are arranged in two rows. The names of the bones in the proximal row, working from the little finger are: *pisiform, triquetrum, lunate, scaphoid.* The distal row consists of: *hamate, capitate, trapezoid, trapezium.*

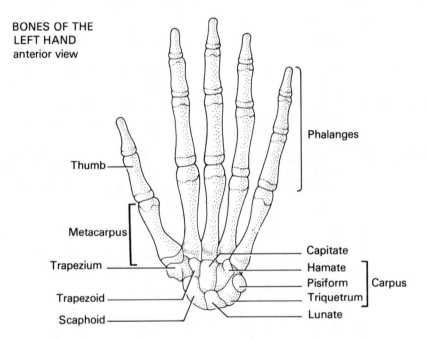

BONES OF THE LEFT HAND anterior view

Thumb
Phalanges
Metacarpus
Trapezium
Capitate
Hamate
Pisiform
Carpus
Trapezoid
Triquetrum
Scaphoid
Lunate

The hand is made up of five *metacarpal* bones. Although small, they are classified as *long bones.* The proximal base of each one articulates with a carpal bone. The round distal head forms the prominence of the knuckle.

The fingers are formed by fourteen *phalanges*: three in each finger and two in the thumb. They are also classified as long bones.

Muscles

There are a number of small muscles in the hand, but the main ones affecting the hand and wrist are:

Flexor Carpi Radialis – flexes the wrist joint.
Extensor Carpi Radialis – extends the wrist.
Flexor Carpi Ulnaris – flexes the wrist joint.
Extensor Carpi Ulnaris – extends the wrist.
Flexor Digitorium – flexes the fingers.
Extensor Digitorium – extends the fingers.

Ligaments

The ligaments of the *flexor* and *extensor digitorium* pass under a strong band of connective tissue, divide, fan out and pass to the tip of each finger.

Arteries

The *radial* and *ulnar arteries* pass down the arm. In the palms, they form two *palmar arches,* a superficial and a deep artery, which give off a number of branches to the digits. There are a large number of *capillaries* all over the hand.

Veins

The veins begin in the *palmar venous arches,* and cross the wrist to fill the *cephalic* and *basilic veins.*

Nerves

The nerves of the hand are supplied by the *ulnar* and *median nerves.*

Digits

In lower animals, the digits of the hand are used for the crudest of gripping purposes, but in man these have become highly developed with a fine coordination of movement.

THE ANKLE AND FOOT

Bones

The bones of the foot fall into three groups corresponding to those of the hand.

The ankle, or tarsus, consists of seven (not eight) small irregular bones. The *talus* articulates with the *tibia* and the *calcaneus,* which is the largest of the tarsal bones, forms the heel bone. The others are the *cuboid,* the *navicular* and the three *cuneiforms, lateral intermediate* and *medial.*

The ball of the foot is formed by five *metatarsal* bones.

The toes are formed by fourteen *phalanges,* two in the big toe and three in each of the others.

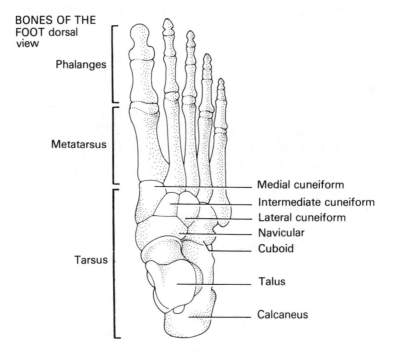

BONES OF THE FOOT dorsal view

Phalanges

Metatarsus

Tarsus

Medial cuneiform
Intermediate cuneiform
Lateral cuneiform
Navicular
Cuboid

Talus

Calcaneus

Muscles

Again there are a number of small muscles affecting the foot. The main ones to be noted are:

Gastrocnemius – flexes the ankle, also the knee. The tendon for this is the *Achilles tendon.*

Flexor Digitorum Longus – flexes the toes.
Extensor Digitorum Longus – extends the toes.

Although there is much less action in the foot than the hand, the muscular actions are similar.

Arteries

The arteries supplying the foot are the *posterior* and *anterior tibial arteries.* These subdivide into the *plantar arches.* Again there are many *capillaries.*

Veins

The veins of the foot run into the *dorsal venous arch,* and thence into the *great* and *small saphenous vein.*

Nerves

The main nerves of the foot are the *medial* and *lateral plantar nerves.*

COMPOSITION OF THE NAILS

Nails are produced by specialised skin cells at the end of the fingers and toes. The hoof and claws of other animals have similar structures. Nails protect the ends of the fingers and form a stiff backing to the soft, sensitive pulp of the fingertips. The stubby finger ends seen in people who continually bite their nails result from the loss of this stiffening.

The appearance of the nails changes with age and with fluctuation in health. In healthy young adults they should be smooth and free from ridges or grooves and should be neither brittle nor too soft. In old age they are likely to be brittle, rather opaque, thickened and roughened.

The nail plate is dead, horny tissue, formed from hard keratinous cells, with little moisture or fat. Nails are transparent so the pink

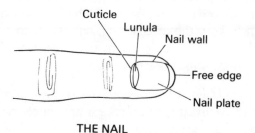

THE NAIL

colour showing through is an indication of good health. A blue colour indicates poor circulation.

The lunula is the whitish area at the base of the nail (*half moon*). The pale appearance is due to the fact that it does not adhere so closely to the underlying tissue. It might be called the 'bridge' between the living matrix and the closely packed layer of cells which comprise the nail plate.

The matrix is the most important part of the nail. It has a large supply of blood vessels and nerves and is where the new cells of the nail plate are formed. Severe damage to the matrix may stop the growth of the new nail.

The nail wall and the *cuticle* form the frame of the *nail plate*. The cuticle must be kept soft and pliable or it will grow up the nail and become swollen. If it adheres to the nail as it grows, it will become stretched and will eventually tear. These tears are known as *hangnails.*

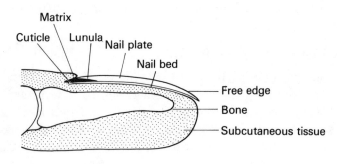

CROSS-SECTION OF THE NAIL

The free edge is the part of the plate which has grown longer than the *nail bed.*

The nail is composed of a heavy material called *keratin* which has a high sulphur content. When this sulphur content is less than normal, the nails tend to split. The strength of the nail depends on the matrix. To help keep the nails strong, one must have sufficient amounts of sulphur, amino acids, phosphates and calcium. These can be obtained from meat, milk, cheese and eggs.

The rate of growth varies but the average is ⅛″ per month. It takes four to six months to produce a new finger nail. The toe nails take longer. Nails grow faster in summer and in young people.

DISORDERS OF HANDS, FEET AND NAILS

Below are listed some terms used to describe various disorders of the hands, feet and nails:

Onychosis – a technical term applied to any disease or disorder of the nails.

Ridges – caused by illness or a deficit in the diet, e.g. a lack of calcium.

Flaking and splitting – may be caused by a poor diet or too much hot water and detergent.

Spoon nails – found in certain cases of anaemia.

Excessively curved nails – are found in some congenital heart conditions.

Leukonychia – white spots on the nail. May be caused by a blow to the nail or the matrix, or by an indifferent diet. They will grow out without treatment.

Whitlow – an infection, usually caused by an injury to the cuticle. It may need lancing and possibly antibiotics, so the patient should be seen by a doctor.

Hangnails – caused by rough treatment and can be cured by constant attention.

Dry and brittle nails – caused by poor diet or poor health. They can be helped by good general care, oiling and attention to diet.

Fungus – a dull yellow patch. It can be highly infectious.

Athlete's foot (tinea pedis) – a fungus infection mainly affecting the foot. It usually starts as itching and sodden white skin between the toes which, if not treated, may develop into cracks and fissures. Small watery blisters may develop. When these dry they form scales. Because of the extreme irritation, the area may be rubbed and so the infection spread to the hands, scalp and elsewhere on the body. Athlete's foot is highly contagious and can be contracted by anyone using the same towels, flooring or even bedding. Everyone should exercise great personal hygiene, particularly at communal swimming pools, shower areas or anywhere people walk barefoot.

For this reason it is extremely important to sterilise all equipment used for any foot treatment. One should never treat anyone suffering from this infection but refer them to their doctor or chiropodist.

Warts (verrucas) – the result of an infection caused by a virus. They are small swellings of the skin. Some have a rough horny surface, others may be pearly smooth. They are sometimes dark in colour. They may be found in clusters or singly. Warts are highly contagious and can be easily contracted from an infected person. A simple treatment by a doctor will usually cure them using freezing (*cryosurgery*) or heat (*diathermy*).

The most common are:

(1) **Verruca vulgaris (common wart)** which is a raised, usually dark, wart found mainly on the hands but sometimes on the face and body.
(2) **Verruca plana (flat wart)** which is small and usually found on the face and hands.
(3) **Verruca plantaris** which is usually found on the soles of the feet and is flattened due to the pressure.

Psoriasis – may affect the nail bed, nail wall or cause 'pitting' of the nail plate. It looks like flaky, silvery scales. Although the cause is unknown it is believed to have an association with a person's nervous state. It should not be treated unless medical approval has been given.

Corns – thickened areas of skin caused by pressure. The aestheticienne should not try to treat them but refer the client to a chiropodist.

GLOSSARY

Articulate   Being slightly or freely movable (such as a bone which is able to move over another)

Digit   A finger or toe

Extend   To stretch

Flex   To bend

Chapter 8

Accessory Organs

HAIR

Hairs are dead keratinised structures. They grow from an indentation of the epidermis known as the *follicle*. The part of the hair that lies above the follicle is the *hair shaft* and the enlarged base encloses the hair *papilla*, through which nourishment essential for hair growth passes from *dermal capillaries*. The hair *bulb* surrounding it is formed from epidermal cells which push downward into the dermis and extend the tube-like follicle as new cells are added to the base of the hair.

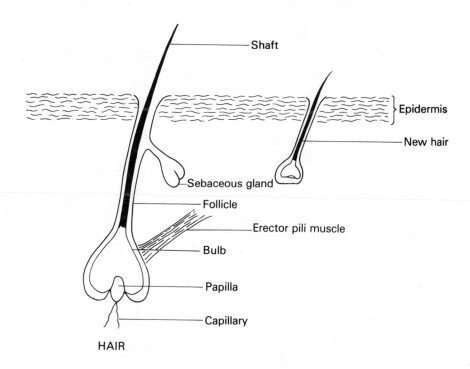

HAIR

Composition of the Hair

Hair consists of three concentric layers:

The Cuticle

The cuticle is the outer layer of overlapping transparent keratin scales.

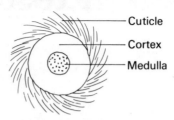

CROSS-SECTION OF A HAIR

The Cortex

The cortex, or middle layer consists of elongated cells which contain the pigment *melanin* which gives the hair its colour. This colour does not always continue to the tip of the hair which may appear colourless as in the case of the eyelashes. Blonde or grey hair has an absence of melanin.

The Medulla

The medulla, or centre layer, is composed of loosely connected keratinised cells interspersed with air cells.

Stages of Hair Growth

There are three stages of hair growth:

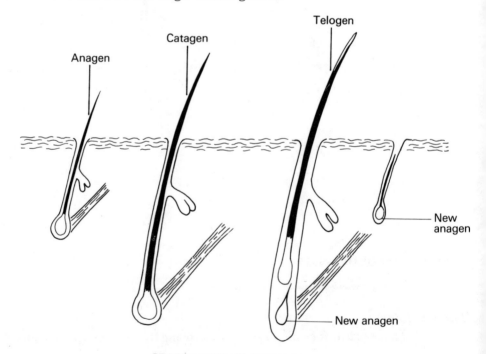

STAGES OF HAIR GROWTH

Anagen

Anagen is the first stage. It is a period of active growth. The follicle extends downwards and hair is formed from the *matrix* (lower part of the bulb). As it starts to grow upwards, the follicle continues to extend downwards until the hair is fully grown. The newer the hair growth, the shallower the follicle is likely to be.

Catagen

Catagen is the next stage. It is a short period of inertia when the papilla separates from the matrix.

Telogen

This is the third stage when the hair is resting, but very often there is a new hair forming underneath the old one.

Classification of Hairs

Hair can be found almost all over the body with the exception of the palms of the hands and the soles of the feet and its distribution will vary from one person to another. Hair is called by a different name on each part of the body:

Capilli – the head;

Barba – the face;

Cilia – the eyelash;

Supercilia – the eyebrows;

Vibrissae – the nostrils;

Tragi – the ears;

Hirci – the armpits;

Pubes – the pubis.

Hair falls into two general classifications:

(1) **vellus** hairs;

(2) **terminal** hairs.

Vellus Hairs

These are soft, downy hairs found on the face and elsewhere on the body. They are usually pale in colour and grow from a shallow follicle. They have a very slow growth rate.

Terminal Hairs

Terminal hairs are coarse and deep-seated with well developed roots and bulbs. They are found on the scalp, eyebrows and lashes, male faces, axilla, pubis and other regions of the body.

Most hair begins as vellus hair and remains so for the rest of its life. Occasionally, vellus hair becomes terminal as on the female face and neck, torso and limbs.

Cause of Hair Growth

The cause of hair growth may be generalised by three main categories:

(1) **congenital** pattern;
(2) **topical** pattern;
(3) **systemic** pattern.

Congenital Pattern

The congenital pattern is inherited from one's parents, each with his or her own genetic structure. This determines whether the hair will be dark or fair, fine or coarse, straight or curly. The pattern will also vary from one ethnic group to another. Anglo-Saxon and Nordic groups from Northern Europe generally have less hair than Mediterranean and Semitic people. Oriental and Mongolian groups have the least hair of all. Usually, white-skinned people will have more hair than dark-skinned people.

The hereditary factor and the general make-up of the genes can produce varying amounts of hair. One family can have an almost total absence of body hair, while another can produce an abundance. If a member of the former family has even an average amount of body or facial hair, to her it would seem excessive.

Topical Pattern

In the topical pattern hair growth can often be increased by an *irritation*. This will result in an increase of blood to the area. Any hair follicle supplied by this increased blood will also receive extra nourishment so that hair will often grow deeper and coarser.

Irritation may be caused, for example, by the chafing of a plaster cast on a limb or the constant scratching or rubbing of an area. It can be produced by X-rays, too much ultraviolet light, and even sunburn. Sportsmen and outdoor workers may develop extra hair, as do many people who continually irritate their skin with too much sunbathing, producing second-degree burning.

Tweezing is another cause of irritation. When hair is pulled out of the growing area, the follicle may be damaged. Each time this happens the follicle will grow a little sturdier, perhaps a little deeper, and the capillary blood supply will increase. What may have started as a light hair growth will become dark, coarse terminal hair.

Waxing has the same effect as tweezing but on a mass scale. All the hairs are removed, giving a bald appearance, but their regrowth will almost certainly be stronger and more distorted. If wax is used on the face there is also the hazard of pulling and stretching the skin.

Shaving removes hair only from above the surface of the skin. It does not get rid of hair permanently. After shaving the hair feels stubbly and uncomfortable. When new, untouched hair grows through the skin it is tapered. Shaved hair has a blunt end. It is much better to cut individual terminal hairs on the face.

Depilatory creams contain chemicals which dissolve the hair above the surface of the skin. They can sometimes cause a rash.

If hair is extensive or dark, bleaching will temporarily hide it.

Systemic Pattern

The systemic causes are those produced by the *endocrine system*. Hormones are excreted by all the endocrine glands and control the growth and development of all parts of the body. If one endocrine gland is not functioning properly it can affect the balance of all the other glands. Endocrine glands are particularly active in puberty, pregnancy and menopause.

The pituitary gland is the most important endocrine gland. It is divided into three *lobes*. The *anterior* lobe is regarded as the 'master gland', controlling the activities of all the other glands. It is responsible for the growth, development and function of all the organs of the body. One of its functions is to secrete three very important hormones:

(1) **gonadotrophins** which regulate the functions and growth of the gonads (sex hormones);
(2) **thyrotrophin** which regulates the activity of the thyroid gland;
(3) **adrenocorticotrophic hormone (ACTH)** which regulates the functions of the adrenal cortex.

The adrenal glands are divided into two parts:

(1) the **medulla** which produces *adrenalin* (epinephrine);
(2) the **cortex** which produces hormones called *steroids*.

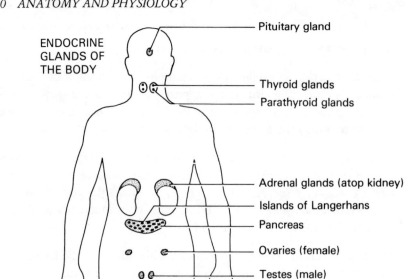

ENDOCRINE
GLANDS OF
THE BODY

Pituitary gland

Thyroid glands
Parathyroid glands

Adrenal glands (atop kidney)
Islands of Langerhans
Pancreas
Ovaries (female)
Testes (male)

There are over thirty steroids divided into two groups:

(1) the **corticosteroids** which include *cortisone* and *hydrocortisone*, and are required by the body so that it can adjust itself to stress conditions;

(2) the **sex hormones** which include both *male hormones* (*androgens*) and *female hormones* (*oestrogen* and *progesterone*). It is the predominance of one set of hormones over another that determines the sex of a person.

The *androgens* (male hormones) are the ones responsible for stimulating the growth of hair on the face and body. A high amount in a man will produce a good growth of hair which is quite acceptable. A high amount in a woman will also produce a good growth of hair but this is not usually desirable.

Certain drugs may interfere with hair growth. *Cortisone* and some *contraceptive pills* may increase growth while other steroids may reduce it.

At the time of puberty the anterior pituitary lobes produce an extra secretion of the *gonadotropic hormones*. These act on the ovaries in a woman and the testes in a man. The adrenal gland will also be producing extra steroids including androgens (male), oestrogens and progesterones (female). Working together these will produce the secondary characteristics. In a woman hair will appear at the axilla and pubis, her breasts will start to enlarge and her body will develop natural fat pads to give her a soft rounded appearance. If she is producing too many androgens, hair may appear on other areas of her body, for example, her face, chest or abdomen. She may have inherited too many androgens which will have the same effect.

In pregnancy, the endocrine glands will also be especially active and often there will be an additional hair growth. After the birth this will usually disappear unless they become terminal hairs.

At menopause the endocrine glands again change. The ovaries, which act on the anterior pituitary lobe, cease to function. As the ovarian hormones have a restraining effect on this lobe, this means that the pituitary hormones will now be free to stimulate the adrenal cortex. This will increase the androgens so that additional facial and body hairs may develop.

We know that the endocrine glands balance one another, that the anterior lobe of the pituitary gland secretes ACTH, which regulates the function of the adrenal cortex. In times of stress the adrenal medulla will produce extra adrenalin. If there is constant stress over a long period the overproduction of adrenalin will stimulate the pituitary to produce ACTH. This will in turn stimulate the adrenal cortex to produce extra hormones, including androgens, so that there may be an increased hair growth.

Excessive Hair

As we have seen, it is normal for women to have hair. But what is normal to some women may be considered superfluous by others. (Superfluous hair is simply hair that is not wanted.) A large number of women at some time in their lives will suffer from what they consider to be an excess of hair. In most cases it will be superfluous hair, that is a normal additional growth following puberty, pregnancy or the menopause.

Hirsutism is a condition when there is an excessive growth of hair on a part of the body not normally covered by hair.

Hypertrichosis is a stronger and more prolific growth than superfluous hair, but still growing in areas that normally produce hair.

THE EYE

The eyes are the organs responsible for transmitting the images of vision to the *optic nerve* and thence to the brain for recognition. They lie in the *orbital cavity* and are protected in this bony cavity by connective tissue and fat.

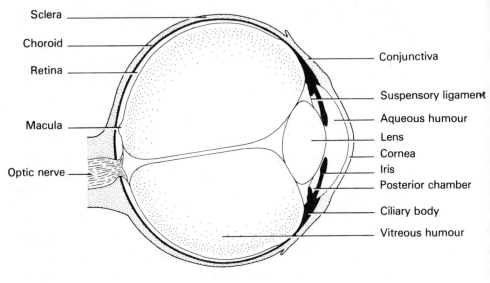

THE EYEBALL

The *eyeballs* are spherical in shape. Their walls are made up of three layers: the *sclera*, the *choroid* and the *retina*. The *iris* is the coloured part and the black circular area in its centre is the *pupil*. The iris dilates or contracts to control the amount of light entering the eye. The eye is moved by six muscles so that it can move in all directions – up, down and sideways.

The eye contains:

(1) the **lens**, a bi-convex body lying behind the iris, which helps to focus images on the optic nerve;

(2) the **aqueous humour**, a watery fluid which fills the eyeball between the *lens* and the *cornea*;

(3) the **vitreous humour,** a jelly-like substance which fills the eyeball behind the lens.

The front of the eyeball is protected by *eyelids* which help to keep out the light, and *eyelashes* to keep out dust and germs. It has a number of small *sebaceous* and *sweat glands.* If one of these glands becomes inflamed the condition is known as a *stye.* The eyelids are lined with a layer of mucus membrane called the *conjunctiva.* An infection of this is called *conjunctivitis* or *pink eye.*

The eye is kept clear by being constantly washed with a *lachrymal fluid* secreted by the *lachrymal gland* which lies above the eye. The tears wash across the eye into a small canal which leads into the nasal duct. If the eyes are not kept moist, they become dry and painful and there is a danger of the eye being scratched by dirt or grit.

THE EAR

The ear can be divided into:

(1) the **external** ear;

(2) the **middle** ear;

(3) the **inner** ear.

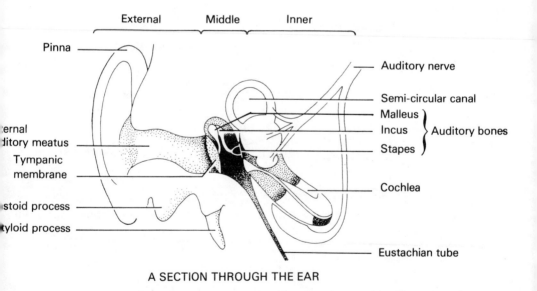

A SECTION THROUGH THE EAR

the external ear is a cartilage covered with skin. Its function is to 'catch' sound and channel it down to . . .

the middle ear. This is a cavity which contains three small (auditory) bones; the *malleus, incus* and *stapes.* These oscillate and conduct sound to . . .

the inner ear. This consists of three *semicircular canals* which help to control balance.

The *eustachian tube* leads from the middle ear to the *nasopharynx* and enables the air pressure on both sides of the eardrum to be equalised.

Sound is transmitted via the *auditory bones* to the *cochlea.* This is filled with fluid and numerous nerve endings. These terminate in the *auditory nerve* which transmits sound to the brain.

The most common disorders of the ear are caused by too much wax or foreign bodies being pushed into the ear.

THE MAMMARY GLANDS

The mammary glands, or *breasts,* consist of connective tissue subdivided into *lobules* consisting of *alveoli* tissue which enlarge to form a reservoir for milk during the period of lactation following childbirth. These open into *lactic ducts* which lead into the *nipple.* They are surrounded by a darker coloured area called the *areola.*

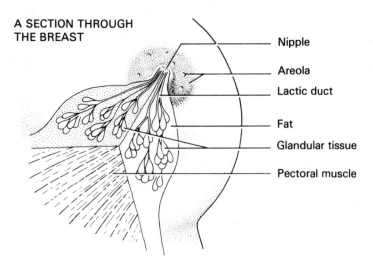

A SECTION THROUGH THE BREAST

- Nipple
- Areola
- Lactic duct
- Fat
- Glandular tissue
- Pectoral muscle

The breasts also consist of a large amount of *fatty tissue*. This varies in quantity from woman to woman. They start to enlarge at puberty, increase during pregnancy and lactation, and atrophy (decrease) in old age.

The breasts contain a large number of *lymphatic vessels* which pass to the *lymph node* in the *axilla*.

The breasts are influenced by hormones: *progesterone* and *oestrogen*, as well as *prolactin* (produced by the pituitary gland) which starts lactation. The *thyroid gland* also causes underdeveloped or overdeveloped breasts.

GLOSSARY

Biconvex   Evenly curved outward on both sides

Contract   To close (e.g. to make the pupil appear smaller)

Dilate   To open (e.g. to make the pupil appear larger)

Lobule   A small lobe

Oscillate   To vibrate

Spherical   Shaped like a sphere (i.e. a ball or globe)

Torso   Trunk of the body

PART B

Treatments

There are many different treatments that an aestheticienne can perform for a client and there are a number of ways that these treatments can be carried out. Some of them are described in the following chapters. The aestheticienne must always be guided by the manufacturer's instructions when using instruments or special preparations.

Chapter 9

Skin Analysis

For the sake of convenience the skin has been divided into three main texture types: *dry, oily* and *normal*. In fact, most skins are a *combination* of these. As the skin is a living organ, it can vary from season to season or even from week to week, depending on the general health of a person as well as on external factors.

In order to care for the skin, the aestheticienne must first ascertain what type of skin she has to work on. To do this, she must thoroughly cleanse the skin and then examine it, using a strong light and, if possible, a magnifying glass.

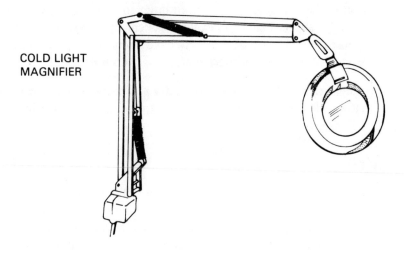

COLD LIGHT
MAGNIFIER

SKIN COLOUR

The first thing to note is the skin colour. This is not just black or white but has many varying tones. It can be pale, 'peaches and cream', various shades of beige, sallow, rosy or even rubicund. It can also be described as yellow or olive, or by different shades of brown and black.

One must also try to find out whether the skin colour has been altered, through exposure to natural sunlight or ultraviolet light. Such exposure will increase the melanin activity and give a tanned effect. Other factors that can affect the skin tone include: drugs, illness and artificial tanning lotions.

SKIN AGEING

Skin ageing is an inevitable process. It can be speeded up through lack of care, too much sunlight, or even excessive central heating. The process can be slowed down by a good skin cleansing routine and regular moisturising.

DRY SKIN

Dry skin is caused by insufficient secretion of sebum. Dehydration – which means too little fluid in the tissues – may be brought about by the ageing process, too much sunlight, the overuse of soap or detergents, or the use of overstrong skin tonic or astringents. Sometimes a lack of Vitamin C in the diet can also contribute to this condition. Dry skin generally has a fine texture, can look and feel tight, has a tendency to flake, and will show lines and wrinkles, particularly around the eyes and mouth, from quite an early age. It will often be sensitive and is likely to develop broken capillaries. It will have an almost transparent look and may have a tendency to allergies. It can react strongly to both internal and external influences.

In maturity, the skin will be extra dry and deeply lined. It will lose its natural elasticity, and, because the fat in the subcutis is being reduced, will lose its firmness.

OILY SKIN

Oily skin is caused by an oversecretion of the sebaceous glands. This condition may be aggravated by overstimulation of these glands either by too harsh cleansing, over heating, often with a lamp or facial sauna, or by a diet containing too much dairy produce, oils and fats, chocolate and sugars.

Sallow or dark-skinned people are most visibly affected. Their skin will look coarse and the pores will often be enlarged with comedones (both blackheads and whiteheads) and closed comedones, spots and blemishes. Often there will be acne. Because there are more fat cells in the subcutis, oily skin will stay young-looking for far longer than other types of skin. It will also have fewer lines and wrinkles. Occasionally too much fat will collect in the tissues giving a 'baggy' look to the face.

NORMAL SKIN

Normal skin will have a fine, even texture and be well moisturised. It will look clear and clean, rarely develop spots and blemishes, have no open pores, greasy areas or dry flaky patches. It will be fine to the touch, with little lining.

COMBINATION SKIN

A combination skin is a mixture of the dry and oily types. There is a T-shaped area of oily skin consisting of forehead, nose and chin. The cheeks, side of face, around the eyes and neck will be dry.

Some skins are damp and moist due to an oversecretion of the sweat glands. It can be caused by nervous tension, fever, hormone imbalance, hot or spicy foods.

Some skin tissues will retain fluid, giving the face a puffy appearance. This is probably caused by poor circulation.

Other skins will be dehydrated. This very often follows fever or a reduction of body fluids, perhaps due to too much slimming or to overexposure to sunlight.

COMMON ALLERGIES

Allergies result from four main causes:

(1) **inhalants**;

(2) **contacts**;

(3) **ingestants**;

(4) **infection**.

Inhalants

Tree, grass and flower pollen and perfume can result in hay fever. The effect of this is a blocked sinus causing pain and headaches, sneezing and running eyes.

Contacts

Dust, animal fur, fabrics, plants and cosmetics may cause some of the same symptoms as in hay fever or eczema.

Ingestants

Food and drinks, anything from strawberries to shell fish, may produce urticaria.

Infection

Medical infection, insect stings or bites may cause both a local swelling or a general oedema.

All these things cause the body to produce antigens, and an allergic reaction will follow.

If a particular product is suspect the simplest way to diagnose an allergy is to ask the client to stop using it for a couple of weeks. If the symptoms clear up, this may have been the cause of the problem. Then if the client wishes to continue with the same product, she can then start to reuse it. If the symptoms return, she should be advised against using it again.

Very often the allergies will be caused by a particular colour, perfume compound or chemical used in one item of a manufacturer's range. It may be in just one lipstick, nail-polish or perfume. Other items in the same range will probably not have any effect.

Chapter 10 — Cleansing

THE BASICS OF CLEANSING

Whatever the colour of the skin or its texture or type, it will always benefit from a good cleansing routine. The aspiring aestheticienne must learn how to perform this smoothly and effortlessly. No facial work of any kind can be commenced until the skin has been thoroughly cleansed.

Dead cells are continually being shed by the skin. Minute particles of dust, natural secretion from the sebaceous and sweat glands, stale make up, all these things help to block the pores, create blackheads and spots, giving a muddy appearance.

Cleansing is the *most important procedure* that the aestheticienne will ever learn. As she gently lifts the waste matter and oils, the skin will start to look fresher and will be able to function more easily.

A good aestheticienne will talk to her client during this time, explaining to her how best to carry out her own cleansing at home. Using her own gentle movements as an example, she can show how carefully one should treat one's own skin.

No matter what the treatment, any movements on the skin must be gentle and controlled. Heavy handling will stretch the skin, cause broken capillaries and overstimulate the sebaceous glands. It will damage the texture and will also be uncomfortable for the client.

SIMPLE CLEANSING

There are many methods of simple cleansing. One school of thought recommends spreading the cleansing milk or cream over the face and then removing it with cotton-wool. Others apply the cleanser to damp cotton-wool and then wipe the face. With this method the cotton-wool is held under the third and fourth fingers of both hands, which are used simultaneously. This allows great mobility and a quick action.

Each tutor will have her favourite method of cleansing. No doubt, her students will adopt their own styles.

Requirements

Whatever method is used, the following items will be required:

Lotions and creams

Cleansing cream

Cleansing milk

Special eye make-up remover

Skin tonic

Mask

Moisturiser

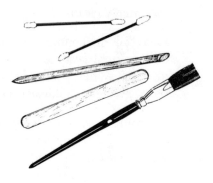

Utensils

Cotton buds

Damp cotton-wool squares

Bowl of warm water

Tissues

Receiver for used equipment

Receiver for waste materials

Mask brush

Equipment

Couch or chair

Trolley

Warm towels or blanket

Head band and cap

Gown

Infrared lamp or cool steamer

Magnifying lamp for inspection

Comedone extractors

Eyebrow forceps

Spatula

Orange stick

Preparation

An aestheticienne should have everything ready before she commences the treatment. It wastes time not to do this and a client who is kept waiting will become irritated.

The client is asked to remove her outer clothing to the waist and put on a gown. She should then be helped onto the couch or chair and warm towels or a blanket put over her. In warm weather or hot countries a cooling fan will be pleasant.

If the client is wearing heavy make-up, apply cleansing cream with the fingers to the throat, cheeks, nose and forehead. Gently massage and leave for a few minutes. While waiting, clean the eyelids.

Method

Cleansing the Eyes

Dip both ends of a cotton-bud into cleansing milk or eye make-up remover. With one hand carefully holding the skin at the eyebrow, gently rotate the cotton-bud down the eyelid and lashes and also under the lower lashes. Repeat until all make-up is removed. Wipe the eyelid with damp cotton-wool, from the inside corner to the outside. Repeat on the other eye. *Do not* use the same cotton-bud or wool on the other eye.

Cleansing the Lips

Put cleansing milk on two pieces of clean cotton-wool and hold one in each hand. Hold one corner of the mouth, and slide the other hand gently across the lips and hold. Repeat, using an area of fresh cotton-wool, and use alternate hands until the lips are clean.

Cleansing the Face

Remove the cleansing cream with a damp pad of cotton-wool in each hand following a set pattern of cleansing. Change the cotton-wool pads frequently until all the cleansing cream is removed. Reapply cleansing cream as necessary.

Cleanse the face with pads of damp cotton-wool and cleansing milk, again following the set pattern. It is important to have sufficient cleansing milk on the cotton-wool so that you can move smoothly over the skin and not drag it. The action must be gentle and even, with no harsh or sudden movement. This routine must be repeated until the skin is absolutely clean.

The cleansing routine should have a soothing effect upon the client. One possible cleansing routine is outlined below:

(1)   Using a gentle stroking action with one hand following the other, wipe upwards over the skin. Work to one side of the neck and then back to the other, finishing at the centre.

(2)   With both hands working in opposition, circle around the point of the chin.

(3)   With both hands working in unison, 'fan' across the cheeks with stroking movement from chin to temple and lightly press; then from the chin to the corner of each eye, and press. Repeat the stroking movements, working inwards towards the nose.

(4)   Using small circular movements work around the corners of the nose. Then use stroking movements up each side of the nose.

(5)   Make a circular movement around the eyes.

(6)   Use a stroking movement with one hand following the other. Work up the centre of the forehead, passing to one side then the other and back to the centre. Gently wipe outwards towards the temples.

Toning

Apply skin tonic to two damp pads of cotton-wool and follow the set pattern for cleansing. Repeat the toning a second time.

Blotting

Take a tissue and spread it across the forehead. Smooth one hand across it to blot the face dry. Peel the tissue off and place it over half the face. Smooth gently around the eye, nose and mouth and across the cheek. Repeat on other side of face. With this method the client can always see out of one eye and doesn't feel 'claustrophobic'.

The skin is now ready for inspection under the magnifying lamp and for whatever treatment is to follow.

Moisturising

If no further treatment is to be given, apply a moisturiser.

FACE MASK

The purpose of applying a mask is to remove surface dirt and dead cells. It may also be used to stimulate and refine the skin, to soothe or nourish, depending on its type or ingredients. It may be applied after cleansing but before other subsequent treatments or at the end of a treatment. The easiest way to apply a mask is with a brush, but this must be washed thoroughly and sterilised after each treatment. The mask must be applied quickly and carefully to the face and neck, avoiding the eyes and the delicate skin underneath them, the nostrils and the mouth. Eyepads should be applied and the client allowed to relax. If the skin is a combination type, more than one mask can be applied at the same time. The mask may be left on for 5–15 minutes depending on the type of mask used and the skin condition. The mask should be removed with damp cotton-wool or sponges rinsed in luke warm water. Care should be taken so as not to get water into the client's eyes, nose or mouth.

Types of Mask

Setting Masks

These often have a basis of *fuller's earth*. They can be made in many colours ranging from off-white to green to brown. Usually they are sold as a mudpack. They should be applied in a thin layer over the required area and allowed to dry. There is no need for the mask to set solid as it becomes quite uncomfortable and more difficult to remove. It should be gently removed when just dry.

Other setting masks may be made from latex or alginates. They are brushed onto the skin, allowed to dry, and then peeled off in one piece.

Non-setting Masks

These masks may be produced as a cream which gently dries and forms a film over the face. Masks made from plants – either fruit or vegetable, or from herbal extracts – usually come into this category.

Contra-indications

(1) Sensitive skins or those prone to allergic reactions.

(2) Areas of sepsis.

(3) Over recent scar tissue.

(4) Over areas of broken capillaries or high vascular condition.

THE LONDON CLEANSE

The London Cleanse is so-called because it was devised to combat the effect of London's heavily polluted atmosphere. It can be used on normal skins in need of a good cleanse, most problem skins and for acne. In fact it can be adapted for almost all skin conditions.

The frequency of treatments for severe acne should be once a week to start with, then once every two weeks, then every three weeks as the condition improves. As a deep cleanse, this treatment can be gently performed less frequently as required.

Method

Clean the face thoroughly with cleansing milk.

Apply a skin tonic.

Apply a skin shampoo with a soft damp brush, using gentle circular movements, all over the face, avoiding the delicate tissue around the eyes, the nostrils and mouth. Go over the worst affected areas thoroughly for 1–3 minutes. If the skin is rubbed too hard or for too long, it is likely to peel or become sore.

Blot with a tissue.

Cleanse at least twice with a special tonic containing a higher acid content until the soapy action has finished.

'Open' the pores by using steam or infrared heat for approximately five minutes. Remember to protect the eyes.

Use a comedone extractor to remove all blackheads, trapped sebum and pus. If you start on a lesion you must make sure that all the waste matter from that spot is drained.

INFRA RED LAMP CLAMPED TO A TABLE

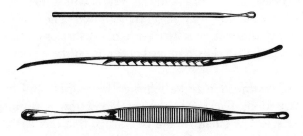

COMEDONE EXTRACTORS

Apply a specially formulated cream all over the face.

Apply a direct high frequency current all over the creamed area for 5–10 minutes, sparking over the worst areas.

Blot the face with tissue, and then apply a skin tonic to remove the cream.

Apply a soft mask and leave on for 7–15 minutes according to the skin condition. Remove with warm water, apply a skin tonic and blot dry.

Apply a moisturiser.

As with all treatments, recommend that no make-up be used for a few hours.

Chapter 11   Exfoliation

Treatment of the skin by exfoliation or peeling has been performed since ancient times. It was used by the Egyptians and later spread around the Mediterranean. The West Indies and Central America also employed this method of skin cleansing.

The treatment consists of removing the outer layer of skin together with dead cells. This can be achieved by applying a solution of either vegetable matter or chemicals which will soften the dead keratinised cells so that they may be gently removed. The alternative method is to remove the dead cells by the use of brushes or pumice. The amount of skin and dead cells removed depends on the process employed.

The treatment may be followed by redness and in some cases pigmentation. This is because the blood flow is stimulated towards the surface. The client should be warned that the iron content of the red corpuscles can be affected by sunlight or a hormone pill and produce a brown pigment for up to six months after treatment.

Exfoliation can be performed in three ways:

(1) by **vegetable (biological)** peeling;
(2) by **chemical (progressive)** peeling;
(3) by **abrasion.**

VEGETABLE (BIOLOGICAL) PEELING

This is a rejuvenating treatment for dry or lined skin. It will lighten sallow or discoloured skins, especially the aftermath of a suntan.

There are a number of proprietary biological peeling agents on the market using many different ingredients. Each tutor will have her favourite. At least one manufacturer uses the extract of the pawpaw fruit. It contains vitamins A, B and C, and the manufacturer claims that it also contains an enzyme which helps to eliminate dead cells.

Treatment should be two or three times a week for a course of ten appointments.

Contra-indications

(1) Extremely dry skin.

(2) Dehydrated skin.

(3) Hypersensitive skin (with extreme caution).

(4) Mature skin.

(5) Crêpy skin.

Method

To start the treatment clean the skin with cleansing milk and skin tonic. Remove all trace of oils with a spirit solution or mild skin shampoo.

The pores may now be 'opened', either with infrared heat or steam, for five minutes. Apply the contents of one ampule of the softening lotion to the skin, and, using a tapotement, pat it into the skin for 3–5 minutes until it is all absorbed. The client may feel a slight irritation at this stage.

Apply the cream mask, avoiding the eyes, nostrils and mouth. Place eyepads over the eyes and allow the client to rest for 15 minutes.

APPLICATION OF CREAM MASK

Remove the mask with warm water and cotton-wool pads using a circular movement.

Dry the skin and massage with a hydrating cream for 20 minutes.

Remove any excess cream with damp cotton-wool, but leave sufficient to act as a moisturiser.

Recommend to the client that make-up should not be applied to the treated area for several hours.

There are many different methods of skin peeling and the aestheticienne should be careful to read the instructions provided by the manufacturer with each product.

CHEMICAL (PROGRESSIVE) PEELING

This treatment is suitable for lessening the effect of coarse open pores, past acne scarring, greasy or sallow skin or discoloured skin (the after-effect of suntan).

This treatment helps to clear the skin but does not get rid of acne scars. It is, however, quite a harsh treatment and can cause skin irritation. The aestheticienne must have a good knowledge of the skin and how it will react to chemicals.

The active ingredient is often resorcinol or salicylic acid but there are several different processes. Treatments should usually be given three times a week or on alternate days. A course will usually consist of ten treatments. The powder may come in five graduated strengths. The aestheticienne starts with the weakest powder (No. 1) and usually increases the strength on alternate treatments. For a mild peeling, she increases only at weekly intervals.

Contra-indications

(1)   Infected skin (vesicles, pustules, etc.).

(2)   Irritated skin.

(3)   Abrasions.

(4)   Sensitive skin.

(5)   Dehydrated skin.

(6)   Mature skin.

Method

Cleanse the skin with cleansing milk and skin tonic.

Remove all trace of oils with a spirit solution or mild skin shampoo.

'Open' the pores using either infrared heat or steam for five minutes.

Apply oil under the eyes to protect the delicate tissue.

Mix the appropriate powder with the active lotion to form a thin paste. Spread evenly all over the face, and neck if required, with a brush, being careful to avoid the delicate skin around the eyes or any skin lesion. Leave on for 5–15 minutes depending on the client's reaction. If a strong irritation is felt, remove the mask at once. Note on the client's card what number powder is being used and how long it is left on for each treatment. If an adverse reaction is noted, do not increase the strength of the powder for the next treatment and decrease the time the paste is left on.

Remove the mask by sponging off with warm water. Dry the skin thoroughly.

Apply a hydrating cream and massage the face for ten minutes using mainly extractive movements (pinching, tapotement, etc.).

Remove the surplus cream, clean with a skin tonic, and dry thoroughly.

As with any treatment, the aestheticienne should recommend that no make-up be applied for several hours.

Always be sure to follow the manufacturer's directions.

Treatment Using Progressive Peeling to Lighten Dark Skins

Clean the skin with cleansing milk, skin tonic and spirit solution or mild skin shampoo.

'Open' the pores with heat or steam and apply oil under eyes.

Commence the course of treatments with a medium strength powder (No. 3). Wait until it is very dry before removing it with a soft brush using circular movements all over the face. Sponge off the remainder of the mask with warm water.

Freshen the skin with rose water or camomile lotion.

On the days when the client is not receiving a treatment she should apply a hydrating cream and massage for quarter of an hour and then remove with a skin tonic.

It must be emphasised that no other cream or oil should be used for the duration of a progressive peeling treatment.

ABRASION

Dermabrasion

This is a method of removing the epidermis by means of metal brushes or grinding discs revolving at high speed. It is a very delicate operation performed by plastic surgeons where the skin has been badly pitted by acne or where there are scars or deep wrinkles. At no time should the aestheticienne try to perform this operation.

Brush Cleansing

The skin may be cleaned with a light brush and a liquid cleanser. With a circular movement and very gentle pressure, the dead cells and surface dirt can be removed. The brushes may be electrical, battery operated or manual. The movement must be very light or too much epidermis will be removed, causing pain or even abrasions.

Some brush sets on the market contain an abrasive pad and pumice. These are far too harsh to use on the face.

Chapter 12

Facial Massage

[handwritten margin notes: 1. Cleansing / 2. improve condition of skin / 3. muscle tone / 4. Balance Natural pH of fluid / 5. cell regeneration / cleansing / 6. Relax & well being.]

The purpose of a facial massage is to cleanse the skin and assist in the removal of impurities by stimulating the circulation. This improves the condition of the skin and increases muscular tone. It also helps to correct the natural oil and fluid balance of the skin and increase cell regeneration. It should relax the client and produce a feeling of well-being. *[handwritten: → skin / muscle tone]*

Many people prefer to use a cream for massage to give a satisfactory 'slip'. This may be unperfumed or contain aromatic oils. Others prefer to use oils. These should not be so light that they run all over the area, nor so heavy that they drag the skin. The most beneficial and the easiest medium to use is a good aromatherapy oil. A special study should be made of these oils before using them regularly.

MASSAGE TECHNIQUES

There are as many different massage techniques as there are tutors. A good aestheticienne will adopt the movements to suit her individual clients but the basic movements will all be the same. They are as follows:

Effleurage

Effleurage may be used over the face, chest, shoulders and neck and can be performed with the palms of the hands. However, digital effleurage may be used over the face. The pressure must be firm but gentle, increasing on the upward movements, decreasing on the downward movements. The depth of pressure may vary depending

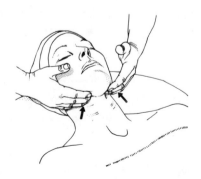

upon which tissue the asetheticienne is working. The hands must move smoothly over the skin and not drag it. An even rhythm must be maintained so that the client initially becomes accustomed to the feel of the aestheticienne's hands and relaxation takes place rapidly. When used after other movements it promotes lymphatic drainage. It is a flowing, stroking movement with no hesitancy or irregularity.

Petrissage

Petrissage helps to eliminate waste products. It is performed with the ball of the fingers and thumbs, not the tips. It is a circular movement on soft tissue lying over bone. The fingers must *not slide* over the skin but *move the tissue* over the bone.

Tapotement

Tapotement (or percussion) is a quick, light movement of the finger tips. It is used to increase the blood supply, stimulate muscles and lessen nervous tension. The rhythm and touch must be even or it will cause irritation.

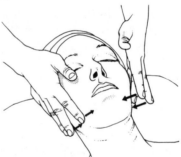

Variations of these movements include the following:

Vibrations

Vibrations have both a stimulating and a relaxing effect on the tissues and can be performed either with the finger tips or the palms of the hands and resemble a fine trembling.

Tapping

Tapping is a form of tapotement usually performed with the tips of the third and fourth fingers along the jawline and on to the buccinator.

Pincement

Pincement, using small and medium pinches, is a form of petrissage. It is an extractive movement which also has a stimulating effect. The skin

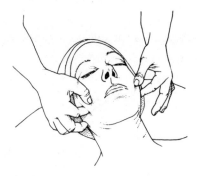

is gently pinched between the fingers and thumbs and released in a rhythmic order.

Forehead Friction

Forehead friction (criss-cross, scissoring, petrissage – known as anti-wrinkle movements) is produced by light movements over the frontalis using the finger tips.

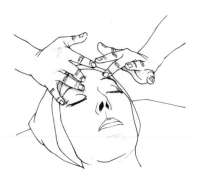

Forehead Effleurage

A soothing effleurage movement can be made with the palms on the frontalis. It consists of sliding up the corrugator and across the frontalis to relieve tension.

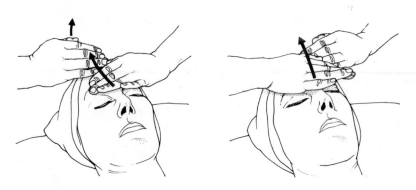

Sliding

Sliding outwards across the cheeks soothes and drains the lymphatic system.

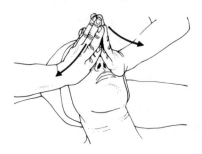

Eye Circling

Circling around the eyes must be a very light movement, following the orbicularis oculi, with a firm lift at the inner corner under the eyesocket.

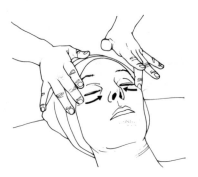

Nose Movements

Small circles and sliding on the nose with finger tips will help to cleanse and stimulate the skin.

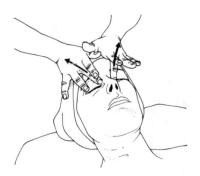

Neck Movements

Movements on the neck include effleurage, tapotement, pincement, knuckling, kneading and gliding.

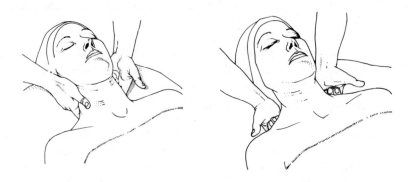

Chest Movements

Movements on the chest include deep sweeping effleurage, kneading on the trapezius and deltoid muscles, petrissage up the spinae erectae and if necessary, stretching the neck.

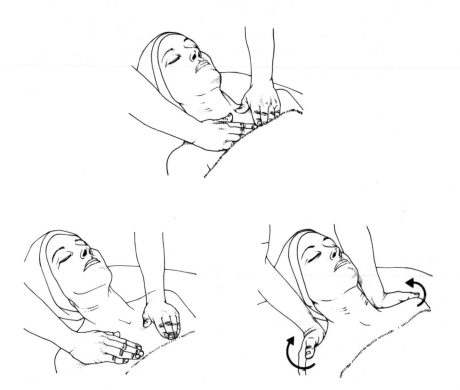

THE MASSAGE

The massage must always commence with effleurage which should continue until the client has relaxed. This is then followed by differing petrissage and tapotement movements working on the different contours and tissues of the face. The massage is concluded with effleurage.

A facial massage should be performed in a quiet, relaxed atmosphere. The aestheticienne must base her massage movements on the requirement of her client, the condition of the skin, muscular tone, vascular condition and the nervous state of the client.

The aestheticienne's hands must be kept flexible so that she can regulate the pressure over the different tissues and maintain an even rhythm. She must develop an acute sense of touch so that she can judge just the right pressure to both stimulate and relax the client.

THE EFFECTS OF MASSAGE

The muscles will be both toned and relaxed. The vascular system should be stimulated so as to remove waste matter as well as bringing extra nourishment and oxygen to the areas being massaged. The lymphatic system will also help to speedily remove fatty tissue and waste matter. The skin will become more supple so that wrinkles and lines are eased away. The nerves of the face will be able to function more easily while tension in the neck and shoulders will be eased.

When facial massage is properly performed, the client should both look and feel better for the experience.

Chapter 13

Electrical Treatments

DESINCRUSTATION AND IONTOPHORESIS

These treatments make use of the *galvanic* current which is a direct current capable of producing a chemical reaction in the skin.

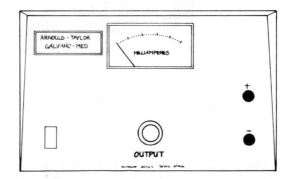

GALVANIC UNIT

All body tissue is made up of thousands of cells. These in turn are composed of atoms. When an atom is charged with electricity it is called an ion. A cation is an ion with a positive charge which is attracted to the cathode (negative) pole. An anion is an ion with a negative charge and is attracted to the anode (positive) pole. The negative and positive poles attract ions which enables a desired substance to be induced into the tissues or an unwanted substance to be drawn out.

In *iontophoresis* the current flows from the negative to the positive pole thus permitting the ions to travel from the positive to the negative position, so that specially manufactured preparations may penetrate deeply *into* the skin. In *desincrustation* the current is reversed so that the impurities, blackheads, sebum and other waste matter can be drawn out of the skin.

There are a number of different electrodes available for galvanic treatment. The client holds the indirect electrode, or a well-protected plate may be placed under her shoulders. The most frequently used electrodes are the rollers – one held in each hand which moves simultaneously over the face with a slow and even rhythm. Disc electrodes of varying sizes should have a protective covering on them. Ball-shaped electrodes or well-protected tweezers are useful for the natural crevices around the nose and chin. The tweezer attachment is

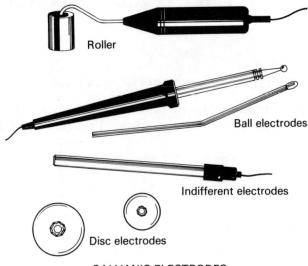

Roller

Ball electrodes

Indifferent electrodes

Disc electrodes

GALVANIC ELECTRODES

used with a pad of cotton wool soaked in a desincrustation or iontophoresis solution. The cotton wool must remain damp. Extra solution may be dropped onto the cotton-wool using a dropper with the free hand.

As an alternative to rollers a full face mask of fabric may be used. This is particularly useful if one wishes to use a liquid as this assists in an even distribution of solution over the face. One must be careful that the client does not suffer a feeling of claustrophobia.

Precautions

In giving galvanic treatment certain precautions should be observed when applying the current. The electrode should be placed on the skin while the current is low. It is then *slowly* turned up until the client feels a *warm pricking sensation* over the face. The current should not register more than *2 milliamps* shown on the milliammeter. The client may feel a metallic taste in her mouth. If she feels any sensation of burning, the current must immediately be lowered.

Contra-indications

Galvanic treatment should not be given over:

(1)   abrasions;
(2)   broken capillaries;
(3)   septic foci.

Method for Iontophoresis

Cleanse the skin thoroughly with cleansing milk and skin tonic, making sure that the face is free from oil. Cover any abrasions and spots with petroleum jelly and do not work over this area.

Apply a film of specially prepared gel all over the area to be worked on.

Give the client the indifferent electrode to hold so that the circuit will be completed. Place one roller (active electrode) on the forehead. (Follow the manufacturer's instructions with regard to the charge of the substance to be introduced.)

Switch on the machine to a low current and increase the current slowly until a warm sensation is felt.

Apply the second roller and keep rolling gently all the time over the area where the gel was applied. Do not let the rollers touch one another.

After five minutes remove one roller, decrease the current and remove the second roller.

Apply more gel, particularly around the nose.

Apply the ball-shaped applicator, increase the current, and move the applicator around the face, particularly around the nose and chin, where blackheads gather and where the roller cannot reach.

After five minutes, decrease the current and then switch off the machine. Remove the indifferent electrode from the client's hand.

Examine the skin under a magnifying lens and use a comedone extractor where necessary.

The next part of the treatment makes use of high frequency.

Apply a special mousse over the face on top of the remaining gel and cover with a square of damp gauze.

Apply the glass mushroom electrode to the face for five minutes.

The combination of the two preparations and the high frequency releases ozone which also helps to cleanse and freshen the skin.

Remove the gauze and all traces of gel with skin tonic and blot the skin dry.

Apply a relaxing lotion all over the face, using a patting movement.

Soak a second piece of gauze in the relaxing lotion and spread over the face, pressing on to the contours of the face.

Leave the client to relax for five minutes.

Remove the gauze and blot the skin dry.

Apply a soft mask, cover the eyes with eyepads and leave client to relax for ten minutes.

Remove the mask with warm water, then apply skin tonic. Blot dry.

Apply a moisturiser.

Advise the client that make-up should not be worn for several hours.

This is just one way to perform this treatment. Always follow the directions of the product and machine manufacturer.

Method for Desincrustation

This is basically the same as for iontophoresis except that the polarity of the electrodes is reversed. A mask or tweezers may be used with a special lotion to draw out impurities.

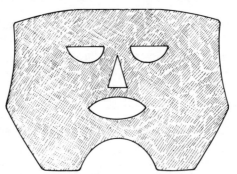

MASK FOR GALVANIC TREATMENT

Combining Desincrustation and Iontophoresis

Usually one may perform *either* iontophoresis *or* desincrustation, but occasionally one may wish to perform *both*. In this case one would always perform desincrustation first to draw out waste matter. Then iontophoresis would be performed so that special solutions can be taken into the skin.

These treatments must *not* be reversed. It is no use 'feeding' the skin and then removing the beneficial lotions!

FARADISM

This treatment is a passive form of exercise. The muscles are made to contract by an electrical current being passed along them. This current is accepted by the body and has no harmful effect if the treatment is carried out correctly.

Passive exercise means that a muscle, or set of muscles, can be moved (shortened) without the conscious effort of the client.

Faradism will do nothing to reduce fat, but by toning the muscles will give the appearance of a slimmer body. In its application on the face it will tighten up sagging muscles, so giving a younger appearance.

There are a number of faradic machines on the market. They range from single-output to multi-output instruments. Some will have a fixed surge rate while others will have a variable rate.

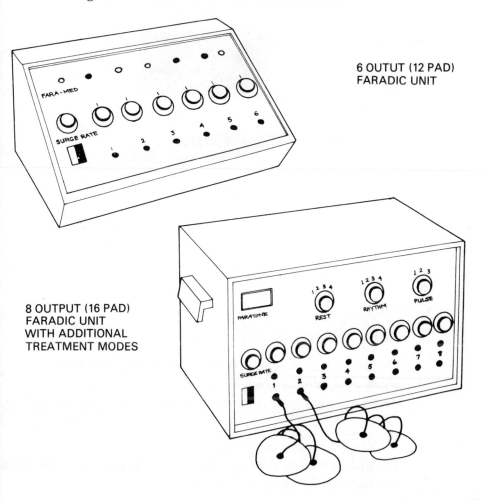

6 OUTUT (12 PAD)
FARADIC UNIT

8 OUTPUT (16 PAD)
FARADIC UNIT
WITH ADDITIONAL
TREATMENT MODES

The pads used nowadays are normally semiconductors with graphite or a similar conductor. They are applied in pairs.

DISC ELECTRODE

The disc electrode is available in a variety of sizes and is mainly used to test individual muscles or to exercise a single muscle.

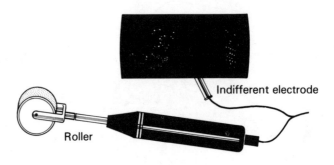

Indifferent electrode

Roller

FARADIC ELECTRODES

The roller electrode is the one most commonly used on the face. It is normally covered with doe skin or lint.

Contra-indications

Faradic treatment should not be given:

(1) over abrasions, septic foci or inflammation of the skin;

(2) near recent scar tissue;

(3) on sensitive skins or highly coloured vascular complexions;

(4) to anyone suffering from a condition which affects the nerves of the face, such as neuralgia or neuritis;

(5) to highly strung or nervous people or those suffering from high blood pressure.

Method

The skin is cleansed and warmed in the usual way.

The machine is switched on but not activated. The surge rate is set to a low rate (35−40 per minute).

The indifferent electrode pad is dampened and placed either under the shoulder or attached to the wrist.

The roller (previously dampened) is placed on the skin.

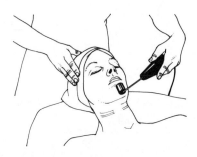

The electrical output is set to zero and switched on. It is then slowly increased until a very slight movement is seen in the muscles.

The roller must move continuously over the lower area of the cheeks, the chin and the neck and not be taken off the skin until the treatment is completed.

Treatment time should start with two minutes on each side of the face and be increased by one minute each side until a minimum of ten minutes is reached. A minimum of ten treatments is required.

Before commencing, the aestheticienne should explain the treatment to the client. The experience − like very strong 'pins and needles' − is not pleasant. It is claimed that some people may find it relaxing, but they are in the minority.

To relax the client after treatment a facial massage should complete the therapy.

VACUUM SUCTION

Vacuum treatment in one form or another has been in use for 2000 years. If performed by a competent therapist the results can be highly beneficial.

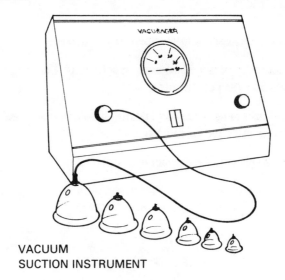

VACUUM
SUCTION INSTRUMENT

Vacuum suction should follow the venous flow or the lymphatic system to the lymph nodes.

The equipment consists of a pump, powered by an electric motor. A tube is attached to the pump and a series of different cups can be fitted to the free end.

The usual round cups are normally made of plexiglass but some special shaped cups are made of glass.

The cups must be thoroughly cleansed after use. The tube may be cleansed by soaking in detergent and then running clean water through it. If performed once a week, this stops the oil adhering to the inside of the tube.

The vacuum is measured on a gauge as a percentage of mercury per inch. The control knob is then turned to the required percentage.

Contra-indications

Vacuum suction treatment on the face should not be used:

(1) over broken capillaries;

(2) on fine or maturing skin;

(3) on loose or stretched skin (after weight loss);

(4) on delicate skin around the eyes;

(5) over infected areas;

(6) near recent scar tissue.

Method

The face is cleansed in the usual way and warmed.

A light oil is applied to the area to be treated.

The glide method of vacuum suction is used with a small round cup. The pressure within the cup is kept low and the amount of skin lifted should not exceed 15%. The movement should be in this order: place the cup on the skin, lift, glide to the lymph node, break the suction by inserting the little finger under the edge of the cup. Never try to pull the cup off. This causes bruising and broken capillaries.

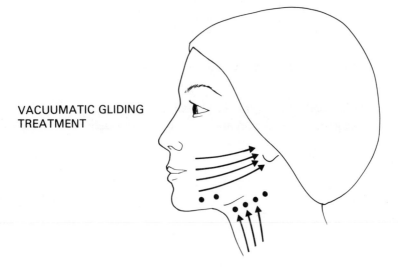

VACUUMATIC GLIDING
TREATMENT

Depending on the area of application the duration of treatment should commence with 3–5 minutes and increase by two minutes a treatment until a maximum of 10–15 minutes is reached. A course should consist of ten treatments, preferably three times a week.

A good facial massage should complete the treatment.

The skin can be stimulated with the glass cups. These usually have a small hole, which when covered with a finger and released again rapidly can cause a pulsation to occur. The effect is rather like tapotement.

A gliding or pulsating movement may be used over the same area.

Skin cleansing can also be performed with a glass applicator, either oval-shaped or with a small round aperture. The vacuum is again

SMALL GLASS CUPS USED FOR FACIAL VACUUM SUCTION

controlled by a finger over a small hole. The aperture is placed over the blackhead and suction applied. The comedone is then extracted.

COMEDONE REMOVER

At all times this treatment must be very carefully performed. Otherwise the client may feel discomfort or even have her skin damaged.

When performed on the face, vacuum suction may be used to improve several conditions; the blood flow is improved bringing oxygen and nourishment to the tissue; fatty deposits can be broken up; the lymph flow is stimulated to remove waste products; lines and wrinkles can be smoothed out; blackheads and debris can be expressed.

FACE LIFTING

There comes a time in every woman's life when she catches sight of herself in a mirror and realises that the years have caught up with her. Her skin has become wrinkled. Her jowl has become heavier.

What can be done to help this woman? The obvious answer is plastic surgery. However, any surgery can be dangerous and should not be entered into lightly.

There are several things that the aestheticienne can do to help. A regular facial massage is the best way to keep the skin soft and supple and can help to keep the wrinkles at bay. Exercising the facial muscles will help them to keep in tone.

The aestheticienne can perform a non-surgical face lift. This treatment can be performed on a person of any age. The results will vary depending on the client's age and condition. For a client aged 30, a course of ten treatments should be sufficient. The result may last as long as six months. For a client aged 55, about twenty treatments would be required, and the result would probably last about four months.

Contra-indications

As for normal vacuum suction, faradism or high frequency.

Method

Cleanse and warm the skin in the usual way. Apply a massage oil to the skin.

Use a small glass vacuum suction cup with a hole to perform a tapotement over the area to be treated.

Change to a very small round cup and continue with the gliding method.

For cheeks and chin commence at four minutes and increase by two minutes a treatment up to twelve minutes.

For treating the cheeks, glide down to the submandibular lymph nodes below the angle of the jaw, or across the cheeks to the anterior auricular nodes.

For a small double chin move the cup up to the submandibular nodes.

For a large double chin move the cup down to the clavicular node and then to the axilla.

Cleanse the skin of oil with a mild spirit solution or skin tonic. Use the faradic current. Dampen the flat electrode and attach to the wrist. Apply the dampened roller to the chin, and keep in motion. Raise the current until there is a very slight movement of the muscles. Keep the surge rate low. Commence the treatment with two minutes each side, increasing by two minutes a day up to a total of ten minutes.

Apply neroli or lemongrass oil to the face and warm the skin with direct high frequency.

Complete the treatment with a good facial massage, mask and moisturiser.

Treatment should be at least three times a week, more if possible in the first week, to be really effective.

BUST TREATMENT

Breasts are primarily made up of fat, lymph glands and vessels, and lactic ducts. They are held in place by the pectoral muscles. They are influenced by hormone activity – the thyroid can lead to too small or too large breasts, the ovaries play a part in their appearance and the pituitary gland produces prolactin which will encourage lactation. When a woman starts to slim she will invariably find that her breasts decrease in size. Other women will feel that they are 'over-endowed' in this part of their anatomy. This is the one attribute that women are particularly sensitive about and they will therefore often consult the aestheticienne about the shape of their breasts.

There are several things that the woman can do for herself. Several forms of exercise can be performed: isometric, resistive with dumbells, or special exercises. There is also water treatment apparatus available. This is rather time-wasting if used in a salon perhaps only twice a week, but can have a good tonic effect if used twice a day at home, preferably using a mixer tap alternating hot and cold water.

A wide variety of treatments can be performed together to tone the breast.

Vacuum Suction, Faradism and High Frequency

Contra-indications

As for normal vacuum suction, faradism and high frequency treatments.

Vacuum suction is a very useful treatment for reducing slightly overlarge breasts. It enables fat to be taken into the axillary lymph nodes, providing the client is on a reducing diet. A little extra fat can also be added to the breasts using this method though this can be quite a lengthy process.

Faradism is used to exercise the muscles and restore muscle tone. The machine is switched on and the surge rate set at between 20 and 50 per minute depending on the physical condition of the client. The dampened pads are applied and held in place by strapping or weighted bags. The current is switched on for the first set of pads and turned up to a point where contractions are visible. These should not be violent as this would cause muscle fatigue. This is repeated with the second set of pads. The length of time per treatment may vary from 10 to 25 minutes.

Method

Warm the area with radiant heat. The area may then be stimulated with a light vibrating machine or manual tapotement *massage.*

Apply *vacuum suction* to reduce or augment the fat. Commence with a low pressure, 6−7 pounds depending on age. Increase by one pound at each treatment, until a maximum of 12−15 pounds is reached, again depending on the client's age and condition.

The duration should start with 15 minutes rising to 25 minutes. A smallish cup should be used only on the area below the nipple.

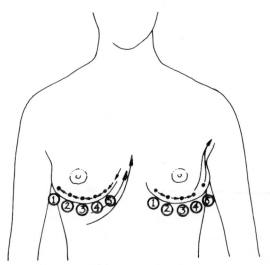

Bust increase   Bust reduction

GLIDE PATTERN FOR VACUUM SUCTION CUP BUST TREATMENTS

Remove all the oil as this acts as an inhibitor to *faradism*. Apply the faradic pads to the pectoral muscles and turn the current up until muscle is just seen to twitch. Maintain for ten minutes.

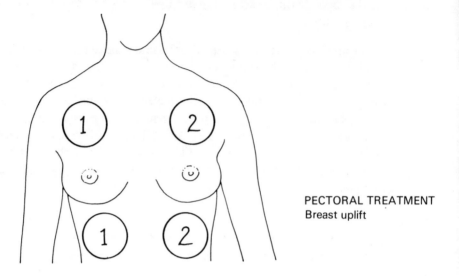

PECTORAL TREATMENT
Breast uplift

Apply a stimulating essential oil – lemongrass is particularly good. Warm and stimulate the tissue with *high frequency,* using the 'mushroom'-shaped electrode or the special shaped electrode. Place this electrode over the nipple, release the air with the pump to create a vacuum. Turn the machine to a low intensity and hold in this position for five minutes. Repeat on the other breast.

Complete the treatment with soothing effleurage movements.

Remove any surplus oil.

Chapter 14

Heat Treatments

ELECTROMAGNETIC WAVES

Everyone feels warmth but it isn't always easy to explain heat and light.

All substances are made up of molecules. These are always in a state of movement. If the substance is heated, the molecules move faster and the substance expands. If the substance is cooled, the molecules move more slowly and the substance contracts.

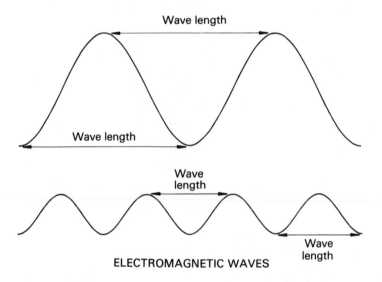

ELECTROMAGNETIC WAVES

Heat, light and sound are transmitted along electromagnetic waves. The length of these waves varies from several kilometres to a fraction of an angstrom unit, although the length of the wave does not vary within its own wave pattern. An angstrom unit (abbreviated as Å) measures one ten-millionth of a millimetre and is the unit by which electromagnetic waves are usually measured. Sometimes the measurement is in nanometres. An angstrom equals a tenth of a nanometre.

Everyone knows the colours of a rainbow – violet, indigo, blue, green, yellow, orange, red. These are known as the colours of the visible spectrum.

95

Ultraviolet rays are beyond the violet waveband. They are invisible to the naked eye, being colder and shorter. When bands of visible light are added, ultraviolet appears as a bluish white light.

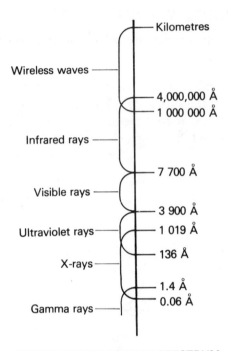

THE ELECTROMAGNETIC SPECTRUM

X-rays are shorter still, and then come gamma rays.

At the longer end of the waveband are the infrared rays. They are sometimes referred to as black heat. When mixed with the visible spectrum they are known as radiant heat.

Beyond the infrared are microwaves and the wireless wavebands.

METHODS OF HEATING THE SKIN

Radiant Heat

One of the simplest ways of warming the skin and thereby 'opening' the pores is by radiant heat. This increases the blood supply to the area, bringing increased nourishment and carrying away waste products. Radiant heat relaxes the muscles, has a soothing effect on the nerves, relaxes the skin and 'opens' the pores.

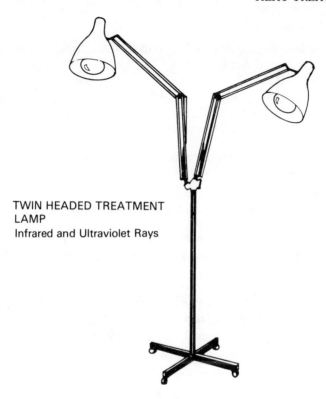

TWIN HEADED TREATMENT
LAMP
Infrared and Ultraviolet Rays

The lamp should be positioned 18–24 inches away from the face. It should be comfortably warm but not hot.

Five minutes is usually sufficient to warm the tissues of the face. If one wishes to dampen the skin as well as to heat it, a lotion may be diffused on to the skin before turning on the lamp.

Precautions

(1) Contact lenses should be removed as they intensify heat and could burn the eyes.

(2) Where there is sensitive skin or broken capillaries, the lamp should be positioned further away.

(3) Prolonged infrared radiation, particularly to the back, may produce headaches.

(4) Superficial burns may occur if the lamp is placed too near the skin (perhaps before the lamp has had time to heat up).

(5) Great care should be taken where there is reduced skin sensitivity as with diabetes.

Steamers

The face may be cleaned by using steam. It helps to relax the skin and assists in the elimination of waste products through perspiration. It 'opens' the pores so that comedones can be removed more easily and improves circulation which will also help to remove impurities.

There are several facial sauna and steamers available.

Facial sauna are usually available from retail outlets. They should be used with great care as some of them may build up a concentration of steam on one area of the face. Unless carefully balanced, there is a danger of them upsetting and spilling boiling water.

Professional steamers are much safer. They comprise a heating element, a container for the water and a nozzle through which the vapour is directed.

The water container should be filled up to its safety mark, preferably with distilled water so as to avoid deposits. Do not use other chemicals or the nozzle may become blocked with the result that the steam will not be diffused evenly.

A 'COOL' STEAMER

Some steamers have bottles into which additional solutions such as skin tonic or rose water can be placed. This mingles with the steam from the main canister, cooling it as it is diffused over the skin.

Contra-indications for Hot Steam

(1) Sensitive skins.

(2) Broken capillaries.

(3) Areas of vascular disturbance such as *Acne Rosacea.*

(4) Areas of broken skin, irritation or abrasion.

(5) Skin having a reduced sensitivity, such as with diabetes.

Method for Hot and Cool Steamers

The steamer usually takes 5–10 minutes to heat up. Care should be taken that the nozzle is pointed away from the client and that she is protected with towels. The eyes should be kept closed and eyepads placed on the eyes to aid relaxation. When the steam starts to be discharged, position the nozzle so that an equal amount of steam is diffused over the face.

Both the distance and length of time depends on the skin type and the apparatus used.

After the treatment, the skin should be blotted dry and the damp towels removed.

Vaporising by Ozone

This treatment is still in current use and is still being taught, although it has been banned in some major countries, notably the United States of America, Australia and the Federal Republic of West Germany. The World Health Organisation states that it has strong carcinogenic associations. We shall not therefore discuss it here.

Other Methods of Heating

Irons

Small irons are available for warming the skin. They are heated on a rod (rather like a heated hair curler).

The aestheticienne must carefully test the heat on her arm.

The iron, which has no sharp edges, can be applied directly on to the skin or over pads of cotton-wool soaked in rose water, antiseptic lotion or a similar solution.

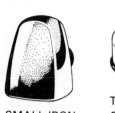

SMALL IRON

THERMOSTATIC HEATER
FOR THE IRON

With this small piece of equipment, either the whole face can be warmed or just a small area.

Towels

Another method of warming the face is with warm towels. These are soaked in very hot water, wrung out tightly and applied to the face, avoiding the eyes and nose. The eyes should be protected with eyepads. When the towels cool down, usually in 2–3 minutes, they are replaced with fresh warm ones.

Thermo-mask

The thermo-mask is new on the market. It consists of electrically heated pads which cover the face and neck and may assist in the absorption of special creams or masks. Treatment time is between 15 and 20 minutes.

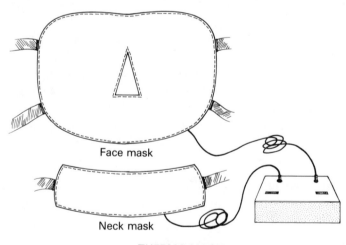

Face mask

Neck mask

THERMO-MASK

HIGH FREQUENCY TREATMENT

High frequency current is an electrical current that oscillates at a high speed. It is passed through an electrode, usually made of glass, which

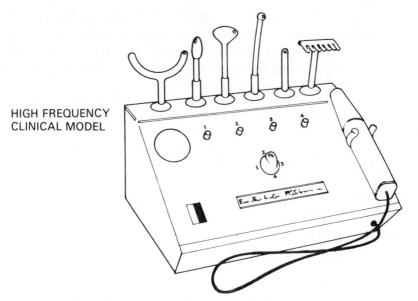

HIGH FREQUENCY
CLINICAL MODEL

contains a gas, argon or neon, which gives it a blue or pinkish light. The oscillation produces an irritating noise which can sometimes be disturbing, so the client's fears must be calmed in order for her to relax.

Electrodes are available in many different shapes and sizes. The most frequently used is the mushroom-shaped electrode. This comes in several sizes. The easiest to use for the face and neck is the smallest.

SMALL MUSHROOM SHAPED GLASS ELECTRODE
FOR HIGH FREQUENCY

The curved electrode is useful for the neck or stroking up the arms. The roller electrode is rolled back and forth over a larger area such as the back. A cup-shaped electrode is used for warming and stimulating the breasts. The saturator electrode is either made of glass with a metal coil inside or is a metal tube. It is held by the client for indirect treatment. There are many other electrodes produced but they are used mainly for medical purposes.

High frequency current can be applied in two ways: **direct** and **indirect** application. **Direct application** is when the electrode is placed directly onto the client's skin. It will create a localised warmth which will have a relaxing effect. It will stimulate the subcutaneous tissue, particularly the blood circulation, so that nutrients are brought to the area and waste matter removed. It produces ozone which will have a germicidal and antibacterial effect that helps dry sebum caused by excessive sebaceous activity.

Indirect application is when the saturator is given to the client to hold while the aestheticienne works over the skin. It will produce a stimulating and warming effect when the aestheticienne is performing light or extractive movements and be relaxing when the movements are deeper and slower. Because low ozone is produced by a chemical change the germicidal and antibacterial effects are lessened.

Contra-indications

(1) Any area of abrasion, rash or recent scar tissue should be avoided.

(2) It is safer not to treat patients who suffer from headaches, high blood pressure, heart conditions, or people with pacemakers.

(3) The treatment should not be given where patients have a number of teeth fillings.

(4) The treatment should not be given over areas of oedema (fluid in the tissues) or blocked sinuses.

Method for Direct Application

Remove all metal jewellery from yourself and the client and ensure that neither will be in contact with any metal. The client must not touch the machine.

Clean the skin in the usual manner. Cover the area to be treated with oil or cream.

Place the electrode on the forehead and switch on the machine. Raise the current to the required level and move the electrode in small circles without taking it off the skin. Do not touch the client or both of you will feel the current.

When the treatment is completed lower the current, remove the electrode and switch off the machine.

Clean off the oil or continue whatever treatment is to follow.

Method for Indirect Application (Viennese Facial)

Remove all metal from the client and yourself. Clean the face and warm it in the usual way. Apply talcum powder to the client's hands and place the saturator in one of them. Apply oil or cream to the face. Place one hand firmly on the client's face and turn on the machine.

Increase the current, but only to the point where the client can still tolerate the sensation.

Massage the face for 8–10 minutes. For extra stimulation use tapotement or extractive movements, otherwise use soothing movements.

Remove one hand and lower the current. Remove the other hand and turn off the machine.

Blot the face with a tissue and apply skin tonic.

Apply a mask and remove it in the usual way.

Apply moisturiser.

ULTRAVIOLET TREATMENT

As stated earlier ultraviolet light is at the shorter end of the electromagnetic waveband. These rays are found between 136 and 3900 Å (angstrom units).

The rays between 2900 Å and 3300 Å are the ones of special benefit as far as the aestheticienne is concerned. At this level the rays can penetrate to the deep layer of the epidermis. It is in this deep layer that the *melanocytes* are found. The ultraviolet rays act on *melanocytes* and produce *melanin.* This pigmentation of the skin will produce the suntan that so many people seek.

Not *everyone* though will produce a pigmentation under an ultraviolet lamp or solarium. What these lamps will do is help to prepare the skin for exposure to natural sunlight. They will also help to preserve a suntan.

Ultraviolet rays will also help the skin to produce vitamin D. This is essential for healthy bones.

SOLARIUM (Ultra-
violet Rays and
Infrared Rays)
Ceiling Fitting

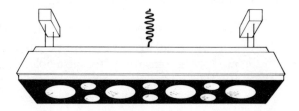

SOLARIUM FLOOR STANDING MODEL

The rays of less than 2900 Å are considered to be germicidal in effect and should not normally be used on the skin. These rays are found only with certain solaria, notably those which have a sliding filter.

Contra-indications

(1) All medical conditions unless specified by a doctor.

(2) Hypersensitive or photosensitive skins which have an adverse reaction to sunlight.

(3) Vitiligo (white patches of skin which have no natural pigmentation), dermatitis or eczema of unknown origin.

(4) Any cardiovascular condition, lung congestion or fever.

(5) Anyone regularly taking drugs, particularly any drugs which produce a sensitivity to ultraviolet light, for example gold, sulphonamides, some tetracyclines, insulin, iodine and thyroid extracts, unless with a doctor's consent.

Method

The time spent under the lamp should always be related to the distance of the lamp to the nearest part of the body, which should be 24 inches away, and to the skin type – best judged by the natural hair colouring.

For the first treatment the following times are recommended:

average skin, mousy hair	2½ minutes each side
light skin, blonde or red hair	2 minutes each side
dark skin, brunette	3 minutes each side

For each subsequent treatment, the time is increased by half a minute for each side up to ten minutes a side.

If there is any strong reaction do not increase the time for the next treatment. If the skin is very delicate, start at half a minute a side. Treatments should be not less often than twice a week and not more often than six times a week. Treatment should not be given if the client is likely to be exposed to natural sunlight on the same day.

The skin should be free of all oils and grease before a treatment. A body lotion or moisturiser should be applied after the session as ultraviolet rays have a slightly drying effect on the skin.

At all times, the client and therapist must wear special protective goggles.

PROTECTIVE DARK GOGGLES

A reaction rather like a mild sunburn may be experienced 4–8 hours after the treatment. If the irritation is severe a mild calamine lotion will cool the skin. This will usually only occur if too long a time is spent under the lamp.

It is advisable for the aestheticienne to stay near the client to make sure that she turns over when she has received the required amount of radiation on one side.

Sun-bed Treatment

The newer method of tanning is using the ultraviolet sun-bed. This consists of a number of ultraviolet tubes under a thick protective layer of glass or plastic. The manufacturers claim that there is no danger of burning, tanning is speeded up and no goggles need be worn. It is nevertheless still advisable for the client and aestheticienne to wear goggles as a safety precaution. A session can last up to an hour.

Overhead Sunroof

Some sunbeds have an overhead sunroof which will cut the treatment time in half. Clients with sensitive skins should start their treatments with half the recommended time and gradually increase it. Clients will usually book 10 or 12 treatments and have two or three sessions a week until they have built up their tan. A well-tanned person will maintain the tan by taking a single session, once a week.

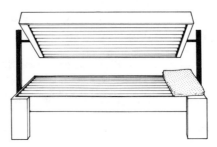

SUNBED WITH OVERHEAD SUNROOF

Rapid Tan

There are now available sunbeds whose manufacturers claim a very rapid rate of tanning, requiring only three or four treatments in two weeks or less. The light is very strong and goggles are ESSENTIAL. They produce a great deal of heat so that clients using them should be frequently observed in case of faintness. A glass of water or fruit juice, either during or after treatment, will be greatly appreciated.

All types of sunbeds produce heat and therefore promote sweating. It is essential to clean the glass with an antiseptic and change the couch covering after every client.

Chapter 15

Manicure and Pedicare

MANICURE

The purpose of a manicure is to keep the hands and nails in good condition.

A manicure will lift the nail wall and cuticle from the nail plate, so reducing the risk of hang nails. Correct nail shaping will help prevent split or torn nails. Fragile nails can be strengthened. Nail varnish or enamels will help to protect the nails. The hand massage will increase the suppleness and flexibility of the hand and wrist. It will increase the circulation of the blood to the hands and thereby improve the texture of the skin.

A good manicure should help the client both to look and feel good.

One method of performing a manicure will be described below although it should be noted that there are many other acceptable procedures.

Requirements for Manicure

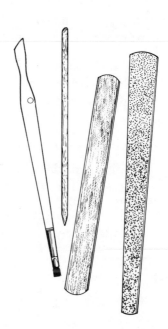

Instruments
Long emery boards
Cuticle knife
Orange sticks
Nail brush
Small nail brush
Hoof stick
Cuticle clippers
Buffer
Small bowl
Receiver for waste
Towels

Materials
Cotton-wool
Nail varnish remover
Liquid soap
Cuticle massage cream
Cuticle remover

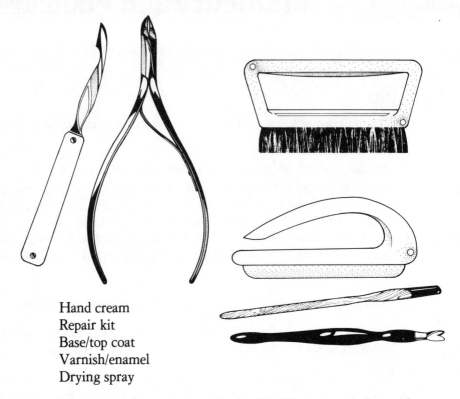

Hand cream
Repair kit
Base/top coat
Varnish/enamel
Drying spray

The equipment and materials should all be kept together, either on a trolley, or in a tray or basket, so that they can all be easily moved to wherever they are required.

The client must be able to sit comfortably with her arms supported. A table should be provided. If this is not possible, a small cushion will help to support the arms.

Contra-indications (for both Manicure and Pedicare)

Any inflammation or infection of the nail wall or cuticle, witlows, nail fungus (athlete's foot), warts or verrucae.

The contra-indications may affect one or two fingers or toes. Treatment may still be performed on the rest of the hand or foot.

Method

Remove the client's rings, watch and bracelets.

Remove old polish from both hands with a pad of cotton-wool soaked in nail varnish remover.

Shape the nails of the left hand with an emery board. Always file from the sides towards the tip to form a curve. Do not file too low at the sides or this will cause the nails to split. When the correct shape is achieved, bevel the free edge to avoid splitting and to remove any roughness.

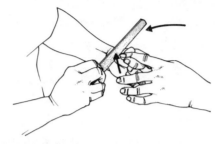

Apply cuticle cream and massage well into the cuticle with the thumbs and fingers. Then soak the client's fingers in a bowl of warm soapy water.

While the left hand is soaking, shape the nails of the right hand.

Apply cuticle cream to the right hand. Soak the right hand in soapy water. Remove the left hand from the water and dry.

Apply a small piece of cotton-wool to an orange stick and dip into cuticle remover. Gently work around the cuticle and nail tips to clean them.

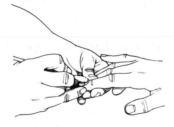

Keeping the cuticle knife wet (with water) gently loosen all the dead tissue remaining on the nail surface and slightly lift the cuticle.

Dip the nail brush into the water and brush the nails towards the cuticle.

Use the small nail brush under the free edge of each nail to clean it.

Dry the nails and gently push the cuticle back with the hoof stick.

Remove any loose cuticle or hang nails with the cuticle clippers. With an emery board, check for rough edges.

Apply a little hand cream or lotion and wrap the hand in a towel.

Remove the right hand from the water, dry it and follow the same procedure as for the left hand.

Massage both hands.

Swab the nails of both hands with nail polish remover and rinse to remove all traces of oil.

Dry the hands.

Buff in one direction. Use a buffing paste if no enamel is to be applied.

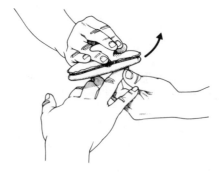

Replace any jewellery previously removed from client.

Use a nail repair kit if required. Nail strengthener may also be applied.

Apply a base coat to the nails of both hands and allow to dry. It should be applied in three or four light strokes from the base to the top.

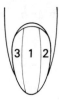

TWO METHODS OF APPLYING NAIL ENAMEL OR BASE COAT

Apply the first coat of enamel in the same manner as the base coat and allow to dry.

Apply a second coat.

If a cream enamel is used, a top coat should be applied. It is not necessary over frosted or pearlised enamels.

Apply the quick-drying spray, directing the spray *away* from the client.

Hand Massage

(Repeat each movement four times.)

Spread hand cream or lotion over the hand and arm.

Perform effleurage over the hand and arm.

Perform petrissage around wrist in four places.

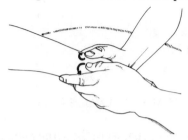

Hold the client's wrist, lock your hand with the client's, stretch the hand, pushing it back, then relax it.

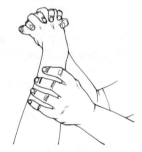

Keeping the locked position, rotate the wrist both ways.

Slide the thumbs upwards between the metacarpels.

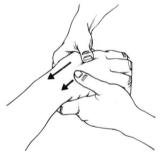

Rotate each finger both ways and stretch them.

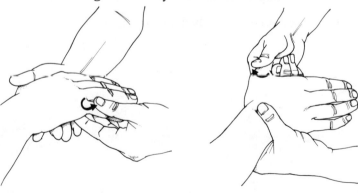

Work the thumbs up the palm of the hand and slide them down the sides.

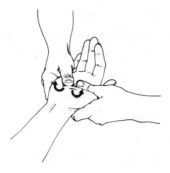

Slide over the whole of the hand, tips of fingers touching, palm over palm, turning on to the thumbs.

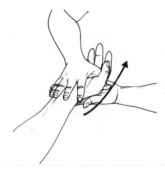

Grasp the thumb and little finger and shake the hand quickly and rhythmically.

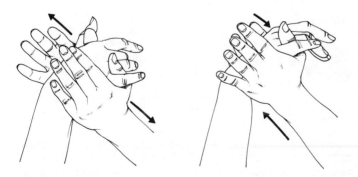

Perform effleurage over the back of the hand and arm, smoothing off any excess cream.

Repeat on the other hand.

PEDICARE

If feet are well cared for, the rest of the body will feel a sense of well-being.

A good pedicare will help to nourish the tissues, improve circulation, which will discourage chilblains, and stimulate the foot and leg muscles.

Requirements for Pedicare

The equipment and materials needed for pedicare are the same as those required for manicure with the addition of a foot bath, antiseptic, and hard-skin remover.

Method

Soak the feet in a foot bath to which an antiseptic has been added. Remove hard skin with one of the patent removers. Remove the feet from the foot bath and dry.

Remove old enamel from both feet and wrap the left foot in a towel.

Shape the nails of the right foot with an emery board. File straight across the nail towards the centre. The nail must not be curved. If necessary use scissors or nail clippers first.

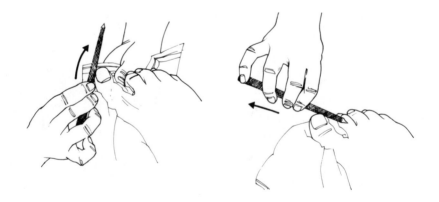

Apply cuticle cream, massaging it well in. Wrap the foot in a towel.

Shape the nails of the left foot

Apply cuticle cream and wrap the foot in a towel.

Return to the right foot. Use an orange stick that has been dipped in cuticle remover to work around the cuticles, gently loosening them and pushing them back.

Gently loosen all the dead tissue around the cuticle with a cuticle knife which is frequently dipped in water.

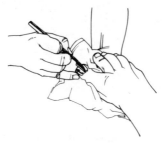

Dip a nail brush in water and brush the cuticle and nails.

Dry the nails and press the cuticles back with a hoof stick.

Remove any loose cuticle with clippers.

Wrap the right foot in a towel and repeat the procedure on the left foot.

Massage both feet and legs.

Swab the toe-nails with nail polish remover to remove any oil.

Apply a tissue or pads between the toes to keep them separated.

Apply a base coat.

Apply two coats of enamel.

If a cream enamel is used, apply a top coat.

Remove the toe pads.

Massage for Pedicare

Apply hand cream or lotion to the foot and leg as far as the knee

Perform effleurage up to the knee.

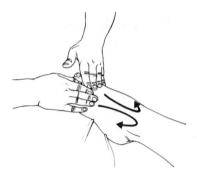

Perform petrissage around the ankle in four positions. Support the leg above the ankle and rotate the foot each way.

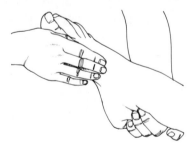

Slide the thumbs upwards between the metatarsels.

Fan out the toes.

Work the thumbs up the sole of the foot and slide them down the sides.

Work around the heel.

Ask the client to keep the foot firm and work your hands briskly up the *gastrocnemius*.

Finish with an effleurage.

Remove any surplus hand cream and wrap the foot in a towel.

Repeat the same movement to the other foot and leg

Many people like to apply a light dusting of talcum powder to the feet to complete this treatment.

PARAFFIN WAX TREATMENT FOR HANDS AND FEET

This treatment is especially beneficial to clients who suffer from a rheumatic condition or who have neglected their hands and feet.

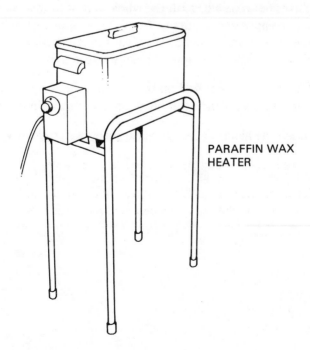

PARAFFIN WAX
HEATER

Contra-indications

Contagious complaints such as athlete's foot, verrucae or ringworm.

Requirements for Paraffin Wax Treatment

The equipment and materials are the same as for a usual manicure or pedicare with the addition of the items listed below:

any nourishing cream;

Epsom salts solution;

paraffin wax in a heater;

brush for wax;

polythene bags.

Method

Soak the hands in a warm Epsom salts solution, or the feet in warm water with antiseptic, for ten minutes.

Dry the hands or feet and apply the nourishing cream.

Apply several layers of wax all over a hand or foot to above the wrist or ankle. This wax must be as hot as the client can comfortably stand. With most heaters it is possible to immerse the whole hand or foot. If this is not possible brush the whole area with wax, allowing it to dry, and reapply several times. Wrap the hand or foot in a polythene bag and wrap it in a towel to keep warm. Repeat with the other limb and leave it wrapped for approximately fifteen minutes.

Unwrap the towel and make sure that the wax has solidified. Work over the wax, which will break up and remain in the polythene bag.

Wash the hands or feet in warm soapy water and dry.

Give a manicure or pedicare in the usual way.

To clean the wax, melt it and strain it through a fine cloth. Wax should never be overheated or melted by direct heat as it is liable to spoil.

Chapter 16

Depilatory Waxing

Waxing is an effective method of removing hair from the legs, the abdomen and under the arms. Some people also use it to remove facial hair, but this is not considered a good idea: it can stretch the skin and cause it to look bald, because all the hairs are removed.

Regrowth will normally take 2–6 weeks depending on how fast the hair grows. More permanent methods of hair removal are discussed in Chapter 17.

After any waxing, antiperspirants, deodorants or perfumed talcum powder should not be used over the area for twelve hours.

The two main methods of waxing are with:

(1) **hot** wax;
(2) **warm** wax.

HOT WAX TREATMENT

The wax should always be heated in a thermostatically controlled heater or, if this is not possible, a double saucepan. On no account should it be melted over a direct heat. The best depilatory wax is made up of beeswax and oils. Any wax will deteriorate if overheated and there is always a danger of it catching fire.

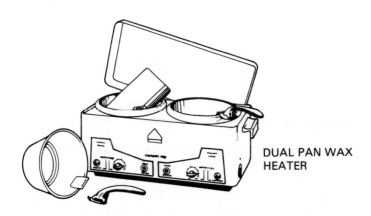

DUAL PAN WAX
HEATER

If new wax alone is used it is too brittle. Old wax is too thick on its own, so new wax should be added to the old wax to keep it at the right consistency.

After each waxing, the wax should be heated and strained through a fine cloth to remove any hairs, dead skin cells and other debris. Do not overheat the wax or it will spoil.

Contra-indications

(1) Any skin disease or abrasion.

(2) Ultrasensitivity, as this treatment can cause some pain or discomfort.

(3) Varicose veins.

(4) Very thin or delicate skin, particularly on an elderly person.

Method

Have the wax already heated and ready for the client. The wax will have reached the correct temperature when it is the consistency of honey and can be tolerated on the wrist. The aestheticienne should always test the wax on her own wrist prior to use on a client.

TESTING TEMPERATURE OF WAX

Protect the couch with polythene sheeting and couch paper. Protect the client's clothing where necessary.

Treat the front of the leg first. Cleanse the area with a spirit solution to remove dead skin cells and oils and allow to dry.

Apply the wax in strips, about two inches wide and of a convenient length. Some people prefer to use a strip four inches long, while others prefer a much longer strip – 10–12 inches. Apply the wax with a brush, first *against* the hair growth and then *with* the hair growth. Apply two or three strips at the same time, approximately two inches apart. The lower edge of each strip should be flicked up to facilitate easy removal.

When the wax has hardened and become opaque rip it off quickly in one strip, *against* the hair growth.

Quickly and firmly place a hand over the area to exclude air and thus stop some of the stinging.

Repeat with other strips and apply further strips of wax until all the hairs have been removed from the front and sides of both legs.

It must be noted that hair does not always grow in the same direction. Wax must *not* be applied *across* the direction of the hair growth.

Some hairs are particularly stubborn and may require a second waxing. Make sure that the wax is still hot enough.

When all hairs have been removed, clean the leg of all wax and loose hair with a spirit solution. Then apply an antiseptic soothing lotion.

Make sure there is no wax on the couch. Assist the client to turn over and repeat the process on the back of the leg.

For bikini line and underarm waxing, the wax must be put on in smaller strips. The skin should be kept taut. The client may be asked to help hold the skin.

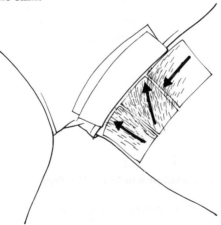

BIKINI LINE WAXING

Sometimes hair does not come out at the first attempt. Do not attempt more than two waxings in these areas as they can become very tender.

WARM WAX TREATMENT

This method of depilatory treatment has several advantages over the use of the hot wax method described above.

(1) Warm wax is more hygienic than hot wax as it is not reused.

(2) There is less danger of burning because the wax is not heated to such a high temperature.

(3) It is less painful.

(4) It has far less odour.

(5) It is far easier to clean the skin after use.

The main disadvantage of warm wax is that very coarse or strong hair may not always be removed by this method.

Contra-indications

The contra-indications are the same as those described for hot wax treatment.

Method

Heat the warm wax, prior to the client's arrival, until it is the consistency of runny honey.

Protect the couch with polythene sheeting and couch paper and protect the client's clothing where necessary.

Treat the front of the leg first. Cut muslin or similar fabric into strips of the correct length for the area to be treated. Wipe the skin with

WARM WAX HEATER

antiseptic lotion to remove dead skin cells and any local bacteria and allow to dry. It is sometimes advisable to apply unperfumed talcum powder to the area. This removes any moisture on the skin so that the wax will coat the hairs but not the skin.

Dip a spatula into the wax. Wipe the underside so that it will not drip.

Apply a very thin film of wax *in the direction* of the hair growth.

Press a strip of the fabric on to the waxed area and rub gently so that the fabric adheres to the wax.

Lift the lower end of the fabric, and with a quick movement pull the fabric *upwards* as near to the skin as possible. Do *not* pull *out* from the skin as this will stretch it. Pull *against* the direction of hair growth.

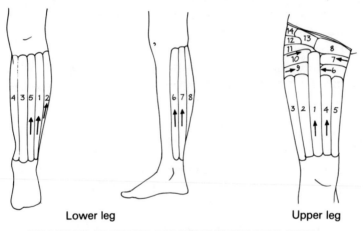

Lower leg   Upper leg

DIRECTION OF STRIPS FOR WARM WAX DEPILATION

Rub the area with the flat of the hand to stop the stinging sensation.

Continue with the next wax strip.

When waxing is completed, any remaining wax may be removed with massage oil (very occasionally this may cause a slight irritation). Clean off with a tissue and cleanse with a spirit solution. Apply an antiseptic soothing lotion if the skin is at all dry or reddened.

Chapter 17

Electrology

This chapter considers more permanent methods of hair removal. They are:

(1) **electrolysis;**
(2) **diathermy epilation (electrolysis);**
(3) **tweezer epilation (electrolysis).**

ELECTROLYSIS

Electrolysis is strictly speaking the removal of hair by the galvanic method (chemical reaction). It is a rather slow cumbersome treatment and, although a very sure method, is not widely practised now. However, the term electrolysis has now come to be widely used to mean hair removed by *electrical* means. This is the only permanent method of removing hair but one cannot say how long it will take and no guarantees should be made.

DIATHERMY EPILATION (ELECTROLYSIS)

Diathermy epilation is the fastest and most popular method of hair removal. It uses a needle and an electric current producing heat.

TWEEZER EPILATION (ELECTROLYSIS)

In tweezer epilation heat is applied to the hair by tweezers. The heat travels down to the root and destroys it. This is a very much slower method of epilation. It is virtually painless, and there is very little danger of scarring. However, it is not suitable for very strong hairs.

NEEDLE STERILISATION

One of the main hazards of electrolysis is the use of a needle that has not been properly sterilised. The usual method is to insert the needle into a pad of cotton-wool soaked with an antiseptic solution. The dial is turned to full or high, and the button depressed and held for ten seconds. This is not a very effective method of sterilisation as it will not kill all bacteria. Cross-infection can be avoided by keeping one needle for each client. However, the needles are still difficult to sterilise, and each time they are put in and taken out of the needle holder they are weakened. Needles can be cleaned and placed in the steriliser but it is doubtful if the normal equipment will really sterilise them. An autoclave is required to make a needle absolutely sterile, but they are very expensive. One way to avoid infection is to have sterile disposable needles, using one for each client. This again is expensive at present.

TREATMENT AREAS

The areas which can be treated include:

(1) The face – chin, above the upper lip, cheeks, forehead, hairline, nape of the neck and throat. Great care should be taken when treating eyebrows, inside the nose, ears or lips.

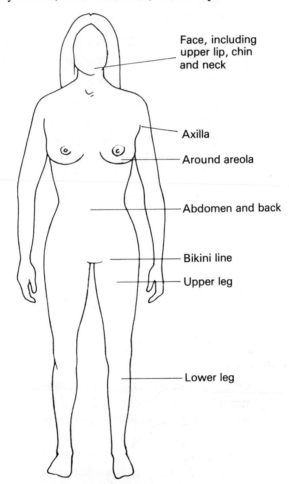

TREATMENT AREAS FOR ELECTROLYSIS

(2) Arms and legs including axilla and the bikini line.

(3) Chest, abdomen, sternum and breasts avoiding the pigmented areas. Do not treat during the last months of pregnancy.

(4) Back. (Note that hair growth on the back is usually caused by glandular disorder.)

Avoid treating any hair emanating from a mole or birth mark, or from mucus membranes or recent scar tissues, as well as those near areas of sepsis.

REASONS FOR SCARRING

Some reasons for scarring include:

(1) Operating too quickly.

(2) Using an imperfect machine.

(3) Using a poor quality needle or one that is bent, blunt or hooked.

(4) Using an incorrectly fitted needle – either too short or too long.

(5) Using a current which is too strong for the area being treated.

(6) Removal of hair from too large an area at one time. It is inadvisable to completely remove all the hair from an area larger than half an inch in diameter in one session. It is better to remove scattered hairs over a larger area.

(7) Introduction of the needle into the hair follicle at the wrong angle – remember not all hair grows straight and some may lie curved under the skin.

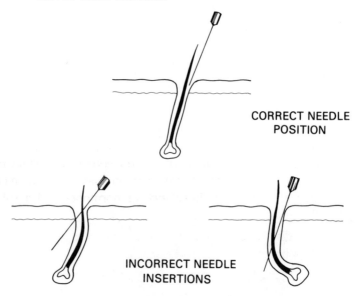

CORRECT NEEDLE POSITION

INCORRECT NEEDLE INSERTIONS

(8) Switching on of the electric current when the needle is inserted or withdrawn from the follicle.

(9) Giving treatment more frequently than every fourteen days over the same area.

Bruising can occur if the needle is inserted into the hair follicle in a faulty manner, too deeply, or at the wrong angle. If one touches small capillaries, blood will be released into the surrounding tissue causing tissue bruising or swelling. It will disappear in a few days.

Some skins are more prone to marking than others. One should be very careful when treating:

(1) Young skin – under seventeen years or elderly fine skins.

(2) Skin which burns easily in the sun, redheads particularly.

(3) Skin with multibruising and poor scar tissue which apparently does not heal easily.

(4) Dark skins – Negroid or Asian skins are very prone to bruising.

The following four pointers will be useful in reducing the likelihood of scarring and ensuring that the treatment will be successful:

(1) Make sure the skin is healthy to start with.

(2) Use a low current.

(3) Treat only at three to four week intervals.

(4) Stress the importance of after-care.

CONSULTATIONS

There are several causes of excessive hair growth as outlined below (for a more detailed analysis, see Chapter 8):

(1) Shock, worry or mental disorder. These often produce superfluous hair on the upper lip and chin.

(2) Drugs and hormone therapy or glandular disturbance. When a woman first starts taking the contraceptive pill she may notice an increase in hair growth. Puberty, pregnancy and the menopause may also cause an imbalance of hormones and a subsequent alteration in hair growth.

(3) Heredity. The general make-up of the genes can produce varying amounts of hair.

(4) Interfering (plucking, waxing) with hair growth.

The electrologist should try to determine the cause of excessive hair growth as this may have a bearing on the successful outcome of her treatment. She should not waste her client's time and money by removing the many fine hairs, but concentrate on the coarse terminal ones.

When giving a consultation look for and record on client's record card:

(1) Type of hair growth:
   (a) colour – dark, fair, red, grey;
   (b) strength – coarse, strong, fine, long;
   (c) extent – dense, scattered, few;
   (d) area – face, body, etc.

(2) The cause of excessive hair and period of growth:
   (a) shock, worry, mental illness;
   (b) climatic change;
   (c) drugs or hormone therapy;
   (d) glandular or hormone disturbance;
   (e) heredity.

(3) Which method of interference was previously used:
   (a) waxing, shaving, plucking;
   (b) date of first interference;
   (c) frequency of interference;
   (d) date of last treatment.

(4) General health:
   (a) disposition – nervous or highly strung;
   (b) diabetes or epilepsy.

(5) General skin condition:
   normal, dry, greasy, spotty, open pored, puffy or scarred from illness or trauma.

(6) Dermatitis:
   (a) a history of dermatitis;
   (b) any allergies – asthma, hay fever, etc.

(7) Scars before treatment due to:
   (a) previous faulty treatment;
   (b) illness, e.g. chicken pox;
   (c) acne.

Always explain that electrolysis is the only permanent cure for excessive hair, that it is a progressive treatment and that each hair has to be treated singly. Some hair, up to 25%, may grow again, but it will be weaker and easier to remove. Unfortunately new hairs may appear at a later date due to hormone activity.

Explain also that all interference must stop except the cutting of long hairs. If necessary the hair may be bleached.

Contra-indications

(1)   Treatment should not be given to:
(a) clients with a cold (to avoid spreading infection on the face).
(b) clients in the last month of pregnancy (for treatment on the breasts and abdomen).
(c) emotionally disturbed patients.

(2)   Clients with diabetes or epilepsy, coloured or sensitive skins, can receive treatment, but extreme caution must be exercised.

(3)   Septic areas must be avoided.

(4)   Hair emanating from a mole.

DIATHERMY EPILATION (ELECTROLYSIS)

Method

First check the equipment.

Help the client on to the couch. See that she is comfortable and warm enough, and offer her dark goggles if working on the face.

Switch on the machine and make sure that the current is not going to be too strong for the client to tolerate although, of course, it must be of sufficient strength to 'kill' the root.

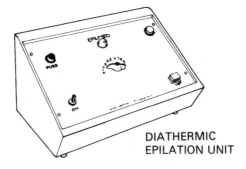

DIATHERMIC
EPILATION UNIT

Sterlise the needle and forceps. Make sure that the diameter of the needle is the correct size.

Cleanse the area to be treated with antiseptic lotion.

Have ready cotton-wool to collect dead hairs.

Use a good light and if possible a magnifying lens.

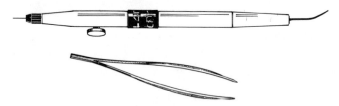

NEEDLE, HOLDER AND FORCEPS FOR DIATHERMY EPILATION

Insert the needle into the hair follicle in the direction in which the hair is growing.

Press the button or foot pedal to release the current for a second or two depending on the hair type and area. If the hair is very strong, press and release the button a couple of times.

Make sure the button is released before withdrawing the needle.

Lift out the dead hair with the forceps. If it does not come easily, repeat the process.

At the end of the treatment, resterilise the needle and switch off the machine.

Bathe the treated area with antiseptic lotion.

If the client wishes to add a little colour, calamine can be applied to the area.

Remind the client of after-care procedures.

Aftercare

For at least 24 hours after treatment the client should apply antiseptic lotion or cream. This will help to sooth any inflamed area and guard against infection. Warn the client that there may be redness and swelling for a few days.

Advise the client not to use make-up over the treated area for at least four hours or, better still, 24 hours.

If the clients finds resistant spots, suggest that she uses the antiseptic lotion more frequently, leaves off her make-up and refrains from touching the area.

Advise the client to leave off make-up over the area before the treatment. This saves your time in cleansing before the treatment and therefore her money.

Chapter 18

Make-up

The art of make-up started in the cradle of civilisation. It is to be seen in the rock drawings of primitive people of France, from early Chinese porcelain, Indian metalwork, Egyptian wall paintings and Italian mosaics. They all show that men as well as women made use of make-up. The kohl used by the Egyptians and the rouge used by the Roman ladies are used in a similar way today.

Make-up today is very much an art and one which can be learnt. In the shops there is such an array of cosmetics that the untrained person will be quite confused. The aestheticienne should be familiar with what is new on the market so that she can advise her clients on the best products to use.

Make-up should always *look* natural. It can be used to emphasise the good points or hide the weak areas of a face. A light tone or highlight will emphasise an area and a darker tone will shade it. If someone has a heavy jawline a darker foundation, or even a blusher blended over it, will act as a camouflage. By emphasising the eyes one can draw the vision upwards and away from the jawline.

Many people believe that one can hide a poor skin with heavy make-up. This is not so. A too-heavy make-up looks unnatural, and will only show up a blemished skin.

Last year's make-up fashion need not of course be the same as this year's. On the other hand, the aestheticienne must always take note of the client's wishes.

APPLICATION OF MAKE-UP

Cleanser

Before one begins a make-up, the face must be thoroughly cleansed and the eyebrows tidied up. The shape of the face must be studied and any irregularities noted. The hairstyle must be taken into account as this could alter the shape of the face. If the make-up is for a special occasion, it is necessary to ascertain the colour of the outfit and whether the client will be under artificial lighting as this can alter the appearance of the make-up.

Ideally, the client should be sitting in a comfortable chair in front of a mirror with a good white light which does not cast shadows. A headband or slide should be used to keep the hair off the client's face.

Moisturiser

After cleansing and toning, a moisturiser must be applied to the whole face and throat. This will act as a barrier between the skin and the make-up so that dirt or make-up will not penetrate the skin. It will prevent the skin from drying out and will form a film so that the foundation will go on easily.

Cover Cream

If there are blemishes, scars or dark tissue under the eyes, a cover cream should be applied and blended over the area before the foundation.

Foundation

The foundation is applied next. It can be either a liquid or a cream, of a very light texture through to a heavy cream. The aestheticienne may use the back of her free hand as a pallet. The colour should be near to the natural skin tone. Two colours may be blended together, or used separately, to lighten or shade an area. The foundation should be blended lightly over the skin with the finger tips. One should then go over it with a damp natural sponge or dry professional sponge with light strokes, so that it is evenly blended all over the face and under the chin.

Powder

Powder is applied next. It is used to 'set' the foundation and may be toned to the foundation or translucent which gives a matt finish but no colour.

Loose powder should be gently pressed on to the skin so that it is caught under the hairs. A clean puff or cotton-wool should be used, working from the neck upwards. The surplus powder should be brushed off with a light, downward movement, taking care not to brush it into any skin creases near the eyes or around the corners of the nose or mouth.

Solid powder may be brushed straight on to the skin.

POWDER BRUSHES AND PUFF

MAKE-UP BRUSHES

Blusher

A *powder* blusher is applied *after* face powder; a cream or *liquid* blusher is applied *before* face powder.

Blusher should be applied just below the cheekbone, no further in than the iris of the eye, no lower than the nose and no higher than the eyebrow.

For a thin face, it should be taken straight out to the hairline. For a fuller face, it may be taken just around the eyes.

TWO METHODS OF BLUSHER AND HIGHLIGHT APPLICATION FOR DIFFERENT FACE SHAPES

For evening or photographic make-up, a highlight may be added to accentuate a brow or cheekbone.

A contour blusher may be used to produce the appearance of cheek hollows or hide a prominent area.

Eye Make-up

Eyebrow Make-up

If the eyebrow needs lengthening or darkening, this may be done with a brow pencil or powder and brush.

EYEBROW PENCILS

Eyeshadow

Eyeshadow is applied next, either with a brush or applicator. Remember that a light colour accentuates and a dark colour gives depth. Eyeshadow will emphasise the eyes and can change the whole look of the face.

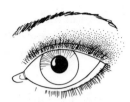 

PROMINENT EYES

Highlight under the brow, deeper shadow on the lid and shading upwards

SMALL EYES

Highlight under the brow. Pale shadow on the lid. Deeper shadow above and in the crease

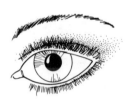

DROOPY EYELIDS

Highlight on the brow, deeper shadow on the lids, winging upwards and out

Eyeshadows come in a wide variety of colours and in a number of forms – liquids, creams, powders or pencils. They can have a matt finish, shine or glitter, or be opaque or iridescent.

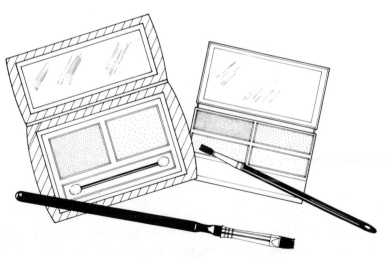

EYESHADOW AND BRUSHES

A pencil should be applied at the outer corner of the eye, in a fine line for three-quarters of the way under the lower lashes and in a wider line for a quarter of the upper lid. It should be smoothed with an applicator until it looks like powder.

A second colour is applied at the inner quarter of the upper lid, in a line from the eye to the eyebrow, and blended across the lid.

A third colour, a highlight, is placed under the outer part of the eyebrow.

A fourth colour is applied to the outer part of the socket crease.

All the colours are then blended together.

A highlight may then be blended on to the centre of the lid.

Eyeliner

Eyeliner may be used if desired. This is one cosmetic which has a variable popularity, depending on the dictates of fashion. It may be applied as a fine line or as a wide one. It comes as a block, a liquid or a pencil.

False Eyelashes

False eyelashes are now attached, if required.

Mascara

The final stage is the application of mascara. This can be applied from a block with a brush or from a container with its own brush or wand.

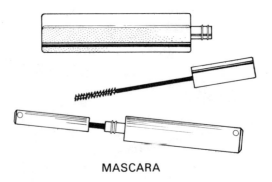

MASCARA

Again there are several colours — black, brown, blue, green or maroon. Some mascaras contain fibres to lengthen the natural lash. These should be used only by people who have no sensitivity or problems with their eyes.

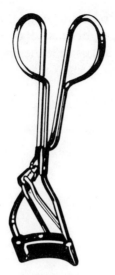

AUTOMATIC EYELASH CURLER

Mascara should first be applied with a downward movement rolling over the lashes and then upwards, coating the lashes evenly and giving them an attractive curve. If necessary an instrument for curling the lashes may be used before applying the mascara.

Lip Make-up

Lipsticks are now made in a mould, in a stick form or as a liquid. They come as cream, gloss or pearlised, in a variety of colours from the nearly white to the very dark.

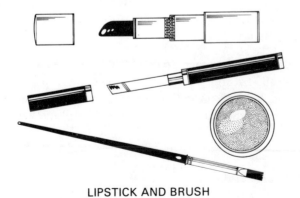

LIPSTICK AND BRUSH

The application of lipstick adds the final touch to the make-up. It completes the picture and balances it.

One must take into consideration the shape and size of the lips. If the lips are small or thin, one may draw a line just outside the natural line. If the lips are too full or wide the line is drawn inside the natural line. However, the natural line suits most women.

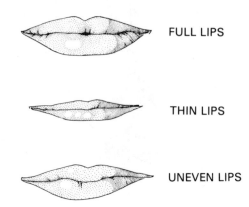

FULL LIPS

THIN LIPS

UNEVEN LIPS

Dark colours will make the lips appear smaller, and bright or light colours will enlarge their appearance. More than one colour may be used to achieve the desired effect, either over one another or outlining each other. The colour must also depend on the colour of the skin and hair. Lipstick with a blue tinge should not be used if the lips are at all blue themselves or if the client has a high colour or florid complexion.

The brown or orange lipsticks do not suit a sallow or olive skin and do not help a 'dingy' skin.

Lipstick should be applied with a brush or pencil. Outline the edge and then fill it in, using short strokes. Blot with a tissue and reapply. Apply a lip gloss if required.

At the end of the make-up check that the face looks symmetrical and, above all, natural. A soft look should be applied for day wear. A heavier, bolder look can be applied for evenings as artificial lighting may blanch the make-up. Remove the headband and lightly dress the hair.

EYEBROW SHAPING

Eyebrows help to define the face and frame the eyes. Well-shaped eyebrows help to give an appearance of good grooming. Their shaping is partly governed by the general shape of the face and by the dictates of fashion.

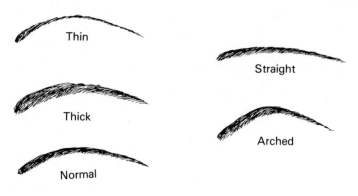

DIFFERENT EYEBROW SHAPES

To shape eyebrows, one must work under a good light and use a pair of forceps (tweezers) that meet well. They can be automatic or plain, either straight, rounded, slanted or pointed.

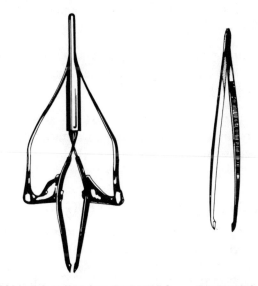

AUTOMATIC EYEBROW TWEEZERS TWEEZERS

Method

Remove all the make-up on and under the brow.

Wipe the forceps with spirit or antiseptic.

Wipe the brow with cotton-wool and antiseptic lotion (wipe frequently during the procedure to remove stray hairs and to cool the brow).

Gently stretch the skin between two fingers, pressing on the skin behind the hair, and pluck in the direction of growth.

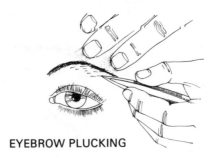

EYEBROW PLUCKING

Hair should be mainly removed from below the brow. Stray hair between the brows and at the temples may be removed as long as they do not form part of the main arch.

Strong, long or discoloured hairs in the brow may be removed if they do not alter the brow line.

Over-plucked or shaved eyebrows should be left and lightly trimmed regularly until a good shape is achieved.

Heavy brows should not be plucked to a fine line in one session. The client should get used to a gradual shaping. It could also be rather painful.

Remember to consult a client as to her wishes. You can always remove further hair if requested, but you cannot replace them if you have removed too many.

EYELASH AND EYEBROW TINTING

Eyebrows help to emphasise facial expression and eyelashes frame the eyes. Permanent tinting will help to enhance the eyes and save the client having to use mascara every day, a particular advantage when on holiday. The tint will last as long as the lashes, about six weeks.

Contra-indications

Eyelash and eyebrow tinting should not be performed on any client with:

(1)   a history of eye sensitivity or allergy;

(2)   septic areas due to poor physical condition.

If the client is new, a 'patch test' should be performed 24–48 hours prior to tinting. This is done by cleansing an area behind one ear and applying the same tint that will be used on the lash or brow. If there is any redness, swelling or irritation over this area this particular tint should not be used. The 'patch test' should be repeated using another make.

Method for Eyebrows

Cleanse both eye areas with cleansing milk or eye cream and then with a mild tonic.

Shape the eyebrows. For students, it is a good idea to leave this until after the tinting so that any reddening caused by the shaping will not be aggravated by the tint.

Surround the eyebrows with a little petroleum jelly.

In a non-metallic dish, mix a little of the tint with a drop of hydrogen peroxide — the percentage varies with different makes of tint. Tints come in several colours — black, brown, blue and grey. Two colours may be blended together to give a muted colour as required.

The tint is applied first to the underhairs and then the top hairs shaping the brow line. The tint can either be applied with a fine brush or a fine orange stick covered with cotton-wool.

Check for colour density after 3–5 minutes. Blonde hair colours rapidly and overtinting will give a harsh appearance. Red hair may take longer to colour. Dark hair will only require a little tint at the ends to even the shading. Ensure that the tint is left on both brows for the same length of time.

After the eyebrows have reached a satisfactory colour, remove the excess tint with a damp cotton-wool pad and make sure that none remains on the skin.

Method for Eyelashes

Apply petroleum jelly in a line on both upper and lower eyelids close to the lashes but not touching the roots.

Place shaped pads of damp cotton-wool under both eyes.

Apply the tint, using a brush or thin orange stick tipped with cotton-wool, over the upper and the lower lashes, working outwards from the roots to the tips.

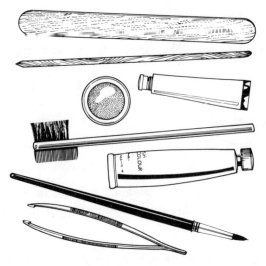

LASH TINTING ACCESSORIES

Cover the eyes with pads of damp cotton-wool. This helps to keep the tint warm and helps the client to relax so that she will not open her eyes.

Test for colour on the first eye after 5–10 minutes. When the desired tone is reached, remove both lower and top pads together in a firm even movement from the outer corner to the inner corner. This will remove most of the excess tint. Remove any remaining tint with damp cotton-wool. Remove the pads from the second eye after the required time.

When both eyelashes and brows are dry, separate them gently with a brush. Apply a little eyeshadow to enhance the lashes which will now appear longer as well as darker.

Always check the manufacturer's instructions as these may vary from product to product.

FALSE EYELASHES

These may be applied in strip form or as semi-permanent individual lashes.

False eyelashes can be extremely effective. They supplement the natural lashes, making them look longer and thicker.

Strip the lashes – i.e. cut a strip slightly less than the natural lashes. If the lashes are new, soak them in warm water to remove the stiffening for a few minutes. Apply surgical adhesive to the lash strip. Allow it to get tacky, and then place it as near as possible to the natural lash line. Blend it into the natural lash, and trim the inner and outer edges. Apply eye make-up

Individual lashes give a more natural look. A surgical adhesive is put on the lower end of the lash which is then attached to the natural lash. The lashes should curl gently. If necessary, use a curling appliance, trim the lashes then apply eye make-up.

The lashes will grow out with the natural lashes. Try not to use mascara as this cannot easily be removed without removing the false lashes.

Chapter 19

Elementary Cosmetic Chemistry – Materials

This is a very wide field, and it takes many years to become an expert. The aestheticienne can only hope to touch on the subject, but she should know a little about the materials that she is going to use.

CLEANSERS

These include soap, cleansing milk and cream, detergents and special lotions. The purpose of a cleanser is to remove dirt, dead skin cells and make-up if it is worn.

Soap

The main constituents of soaps are either animal fats or vegetable oils neutralised by an alkali. They usually contain a perfume.

On the delicate facial skin any free alkali can sometimes prove too strong and cause dry patches on the skin. Perfume compounds can cause allergic reaction in some people. It is not a good idea to recommend the use of soap on the face. It must be very thoroughly rinsed off if it is used. As a cleansing agent it does not remove the deep seated dirt on the face. It is much better to freshen the face with warm water and then use other cleansers.

However, soap and water should be used over the rest of the body daily.

Cleansing Cream

This includes cold cream which was originally made by Galen for the ladies of Ancient Greece. Modern cleansing creams contain oils and wax to form an emollient. Water is added if the cream is emulsified. It should spread easily over the skin, dissolving make-up and dislodging dirt and dead skin cells so that it can easily be removed with damp cotton wool.

Cleansing Milk

Cleansing milks are mainly made of oil and water emulsions. They will spread easily and penetrate a little deeper than cleansing cream. They will lift out dirt and dead skin cells without dragging the skin, but will take a little longer to remove make-up than cleansing cream.

Detergent Cleansers

Detergent cleansers are modern synthetics and can be used in place of soap. In most cases they are very mild and do no harm to the skin. They include soapless lather cleansers which are particularly good for cleansing an oily or blemished skin.

Oil Cleansers

Oil cleansers are suitable for removing eye make-up.

Pads

Pads, soaked in either a cleansing cream or milk are sold commercially.

TONING LOTIONS

These are used to tone or freshen the skin after cleansing and to remove the residue of the cleanser.

Flower Waters

The mildest toners are the flower waters. Rose and camomile are very popular. They are more suitable for dry and sensitive skins.

Skin Tonics

These are a little stronger and will contain some spirit as well as water and perfume. They may also contain camphor or witch-hazel which will stimulate the circulation and close the pores. They are suitable for the normal or combination type of skin.

Astringents

These contain added ingredients. These may include zinc sulphate, herbal compounds or tannic acid, all of which have skin tightening properties. They are suitable for the oily or heavy mature skin.

Antiseptics

These come in cream or lotion form. The lotions should counteract the spread of infection. Some ointments may be produced to dry up spots while creams are used to hide them.

MOISTURISERS

These are made as creams or lotions. Most moisturisers will form a barrier slowing down the moisture loss from the skin and prohibiting particles of make-up or dirt from entering it. They may contain glycerine, sorbitol or polyethylene glycol among other ingredients. They will attract water and hold it. This is particularly useful in hot climates or in centrally-heated houses and also as a protection against cold or wet weather.

MASKS

The purpose of a mask is to cleanse the skin. This it does by forming a film over the skin and excluding air. This causes the skin to perspire, thereby throwing out impurities.

There are several kinds of masks:

Melted Paraffin Wax

Melted paraffin wax spread over the face with a brush will cause perspiration and help to remove dirt and impurities.

Latex Rubber

Masks made up of latex rubber will have a similar action as melted paraffin wax.

Plastics

Other masks will use gums or gelatines or the newer synthetics such as polyethylene glycol with polyvinyl which will form a fine skin.

Mud Pack

One of the oldest forms of the mask is the mud pack. As this dries on the face it hardens and gives the sensation of tightening the skin.

Clay

Other masks consist of mineral earth such as china clay, kaolin, Fullers' earth or bentonite mixed with glycerine or water. These form a solid mask on the face.

Cream

Some masks are formulated so as not to form a solid mass but to stay as a cream. These are much easier to apply and also to remove.

NIGHT CREAMS

There are two ways to help combat dry skin – to prevent the water loss from the skin, so permitting fluid to accumulate in the tissues, or by attracting moisture from the atmosphere into the tissues. The latter is usually called a *moisturiser* and the former will normally be employed as a *night cream*.

Night Cream

One of the best constituents for a night cream is lanolin. This is a natural oil secreted by sheep to keep their wool soft in much the same way as humans secrete sebum. There are several grades of quality. A number of people will claim to be allergic to lanolin. They may in fact be allergic to the impurities in low-grade qualities. When the best quality is used very few people show any reaction.

A night moisturising cream should be gently applied to the skin, left for ten minutes and the surplus cream blotted off. This will leave the skin soft and non-greasy while permitting it to absorb all the nutrients required.

MASSAGE CREAMS

The purpose of these oils and creams is to allow the aestheticienne's hands to slide easily over the face and body of the client.

Cleansing and Cold Creams

Some cleansing creams or cold creams are ideal for massage work, others are especially produced and can be unperfumed or contain essential oils.

Massage Oils

Ordinary massage oil is usually of mineral origin with perfume and colour added. Some manufacturers will add a percentage of vegetable oil. This will make it a little heavier and easier to use.

Essential Oils

Essential oils are the pure extracts of plants and herbs. Each one has its own known therapeutic dosage. As the percentage to be used will differ widely with each oil, it is not a good idea to mix one's own oils unless one has an extensive knowledge of them. Pure essential oils are very costly and the aestheticienne can waste a lot of money trying to blend them herself.

Essential oils used for aromatheraphy should always have a vegetable oil as a carrier. The most expensive used will be avocado, almond and peach kernel oil. Wheat germ oil is particularly suitable as it also adds Vitamin E to the surface of the skin.

Some people blending their own oils have been known to use commercial cooking oils. This is not recommended as their viscosity is too heavy and there is a tendency for them to have an unpleasant odour.

All vegetable oils will eventually go rancid, some quicker than others. It is well worth buying from a reputable manufacturer who will know not only the right dosage of each essential oil but the best carrier for it.

CREAMS FOR MATURE SKINS

Hormone Creams

Hormone creams are aimed at replacing the natural supply of oestrogen which decreases in the body after a women reaches the menopause. These can now be reproduced synthetically. It is interesting to note that hormone preparations have been banned in some countries, on the grounds that if the dosage is to be of any use there can be side-effects such as superfluous hair growth or in some cases skin carcinoma. In the United Kingdom only 0.004% of hormone compound may be used in a preparation.

Placenta Creams

Placenta creams are claimed to have a rejuvenating effect on mature skins. In most cases bovine placenta is used, that is, the placenta of a new-born calf. However, at least one firm proudly claims to use human placentae.

Collagen

Collagen is the name given to the connective fibres interweaving with the skin cells giving it elasticity. Some manufacturers claim to have isolated the essential protein compound and to be able to replace it in skins which have lost their natural elasticity either through natural ageing or too much exposure to ultraviolet (artificial or sun) light.

Vitamin Creams

Vitamin creams are harmless in use and can even have a beneficial effect. Vitamin E is known for its rejuvenating effect upon the surface of the skin.

Some people have tried opening Vitamen E capsules and spreading the oil over their face. This oil is very heavy and is apt to drag the skin. A light Vitamin E oil will be absorbed and is said to be good for healing superficial scar tissue.

Pollen Creams

Pollen can be collected in two ways: by brushing it straight from the plants or from the legs of bees as they go into the hive. For those people who are allergic to pollen, products made from pollen collected in the first way can be rather unpleasant. However, when bees carry pollen on their legs, it undergoes a chemical change, which usually reduces the allergic factor for even the most sensitive people. Creams or lotions made from this pollen can have a very beneficial effect upon the skin, possibly because it is high in Vitamin B.

A topical application of honey or royal jelly is of very little benefit to the skin. It is better taken internally.

Non-commercial Creams

Some aestheticiennes may wish to prepare their own skin creams. These may include such varied delights as eggs, honey, cucumber, oatmeal, strawberries and yoghurt. Lotions may include rose water, lemon juice and milk.

It must be remembered that any commercially produced product will contain some form of preservative in order to keep it in a good condition and prevent it becoming rancid or growing bacteria. People who make their own products will not normally be able to add natural preservatives. Their preparations will only be able to be kept for a couple of days at most. This makes them very expensive to produce.

PART C
Salon Management

It is possible to train almost any person to become an aestheticienne, but it takes something more to turn her into a good one.

She will have to learn how to observe people: how they sit, whether they are relaxed or tense, if they have any skin problem, the condition of their hands, whether they need electrolysis, and many other points.

She will need to learn how to communicate with people, how to help them to relax so that they can discuss their particular problem.

In short, she must learn how she can best help her clients.

I hope that the following chapters will assist the student to gain a better understanding of her clients and so help her to become a successful, caring and responsible aestheticienne.

Chapter 20

The Client

RECEPTION

At all times the comfort and care of the client is paramount. She must be made to feel welcome as soon as she enters the salon.

A woman will usually come to a clinic because she needs help. She may have unwanted hair. She may suffer from tension. She may be overweight. She has a problem and she requires help. It is not enough merely to perform electrolysis, a massage or a faradic treatment. She must be helped to understand her problem and how it can be treated. She will need understanding and even sympathy.

For her unwanted hair, she should be told a little of how the hair grows and how electrolysis can help her. She should also be told that it can be painful. A good electrologist, however, will be able to minimise this discomfort both by her techniques and by her sympathetic attitude.

A relaxing massage or facial can help to alleviate tension. By asking the right questions and carefully listening to the answers, a good aestheticienne can very often pinpoint the cause of the tension and so may help the client to avoid, or at least lessen, it in the future.

With the overweight client, the aestheticienne must first win her cooperation and then try to find out when and why she first became overweight. She must then persuade her to go on a reducing diet. Only after that is it time to discuss what her specific treatment should be.

The aestheticienne must build up the confidence of the client. Where possible the client should always be seen by the same aestheticienne at each appointment so as to maintain continuity of treatment. If the client sees a new person each time, she may lose her confidence and not bother to continue her treatment.

Where possible the client should enjoy her treatment and look forward to her next visit. She must have confidence in her aestheticienne and respect for her knowledge, realising that the treatment she is receiving is correct for her. She must feel that she is receiving value for money, both in time and treatment.

Obviously the client must never be embarrassed by word or action. For example, an aestheticienne must not tell a client that she is 'fat', but that perhaps that she may be a little 'overweight'.

An aestheticienne will become used to seeing people unclothed. The client, however, may feel a sense of modesty in undressing before another person. Her privacy must be observed when disrobing. A gown or towels must be provided to cover her. The client must be clearly instructed on how much clothing she should remove.

The client must be helped on to the couch, covered up and made as comfortable as possible. A loosely-rolled towel placed under the small of the back can sometimes relieve back tension.

At all times the client must be kept warm. In hot weather the atmosphere should be cooled as much as possible without 'chilling' the client.

RECORD CARD

It is an essential part of the aestheticienne's work to keep a record not only of her clients but of their progress.

Name	Address
Sex ___ Age ___	
Doctor's Name ___	
Telephone No. ___	Home ___
	Telephone No. Work ___
Medical History	

Date	Treatment Received	Other relevant details

The details should include name, address, phone number (daytime number if working as well as home number), age, sex, reason for visit and any general observations. It should be noted whether the client suffers from diabetes, epilepsy, cardiac or upper respiratory problems.

Recent surgery, and any other relevant medical data should also be noted. These last details need not necessarily be obtained at the consultation but may be added to the card as the information is volunteered by the client. In some cases the name and address of **the doctor** may be added when available.

After each visit, the date and the treatment given should be noted. Extra details may also be added – e.g., for a face treatment, the client's skin type; for hand treatment, the condition of the nails.

CONSULTATION

The consultation usually takes place the first time that the client meets the aestheticienne. It is important to make a good impression on the prospective client and to create an air of confidence. Professionalism is the keynote. The aestheticienne should be able to discuss and to advise on what she feels is the best treatment for that client. It may not be quite what the client envisaged, but if she is persuaded that this is the treatment that she requires, she will usually readily concur.

The client must be left in no doubt as to the full cost of the treatment or series of treatments. She should be informed if there are any extras. She should never be presented with a bill for the treatment plus a host of hidden extras. This will only embarrass her. There must, of course, be complete honesty on the part of the aestheticienne. She must not recommend an expensive treatment when a cheaper treatment would serve the condition just as well.

During the consultation the client should have details of the treatment explained to her and have the opportunity to ask questions.

At the end of the consultation the client should feel confidence in the aestheticienne and look forward to her treatment.

In some cases it is advisable for the treatment to follow on after the consultation. Occasionally the client will go home, and because she is unsure of the treatment, may change her mind and cancel. If she has had one treatment, and enjoyed it, she will willingly return for others.

Chapter 21

The Salon

When an aestheticiene has just qualified there are many avenues open to her.

She may wish to gain experience in a salon, save a little money and then branch out on her own. A number of aestheticiennes operate a home visiting practice. Very little equipment is required to start, although transport is essential. Others use a spare room in their own homes, again starting with the minimum amount of equipment.

If one has capital, it is worthwhile investing it in larger premises or more equipment, gradually building up a regular clientele and then taking on a reliable assistant. A word of caution: the work may be seasonal so it is advisable not to overcapitalise in equipment or to overstaff.

SETTING UP A SALON

Whether one is setting up a large salon or a small clinic, there are many points to be considered.

Premises

First you must find suitable premises for the type of salon you wish to establish. This may be a room in your own home, a shop in the high street or a mansion for a health farm.

It is advisable not to purchase or lease any property without consulting the local planning department or similar authority. They may refuse to permit a change of usage, that is, to turn part of a residential house into a salon, or a grocery into a clinic. They may also refuse permission if they feel that there are too many similar establishments in the area and not enough shops.

Once you have found your property and obtained planning permission it will usually have to be inspected by the local health authority, the fire prevention officer and back to the planning department if you wish to make structural alterations.

Licence

Most countries require an aestheticienne to have a licence to practise. It will be issued only for those areas in which she is trained. They will also insist that she has qualified from an establishment recognised by them or holding an examination diploma from an acceptable examining board. The council will wish to see the diplomas and certificates and usually insist that some are on public view.

The local council may have certain regulations regarding advertising, publication of treatments and prices, and safety regulations.

Inspectors appointed by the local council have the automatic right to call at the premises to see that all the conditions are being complied with. They may enter at any time during normal working hours.

As well as inspecting the premises for hygiene purposes, noting toilet and washing facilities, the council may examine equipment for safety, and check on fire extinguishers and first aid boxes, to see if they are adequate. They may check the temperature of the treatment rooms to see if they are warm enough. They may question how and where laundry is done, how waste material is disposed of and what form of steriliser is used.

In certain parts of the world there is an unfortunate impression that a 'school' does not give as good tuition as a 'college', that a 'school' is for young children and a 'college' is for adults. In the United Kingdom this is not necessarily correct; there are both good and poor schools and colleges giving training in aesthetics and beauty therapy.

Insurance

Once you have obtained the necessary licence, the next step is to make sure that the premises and contents are adequately insured. As you add extra equipment you should notify the insurers. It is also essential to have a third party insurance to cover clients having an accident on the premises not related to their treatment. You must also carry a professional indemnity, for yourself and all staff, to cover any accident or mishap to a client during or pertaining to a treatment.

Accounts

Most countries expect accounts of payments received and expenses to be kept for tax purposes. Usually a simple accounting system is sufficient, but unless one already has knowledge of what is required, it is a good idea to seek advice from an accountant.

DESIGNING A SALON

When planning a salon, one must make the best use of all available space. You must first consider how much money you have available to make purchases, then what range of treatments you wish to give. This will give you a guide as to what equipment is required.

Reception Area

The reception area must be well-appointed, with comfortable chairs for the clients, a rack for magazines, a table for flowers, coffee cups and ash trays, a desk for the receptionist, and display cabinets for make-up and lotions for sale.

Changing Room

There must be a toilet and washing facilities for clients as well as somewhere to hang their coats. Individual changing rooms are preferred by most people. These should be well lit, and have a mirror and a chair so that the client can make up after a treatment if she so wishes. Complimentary cleansers, cotton-wool and tissues are appreciated. Lockable cupboards should be provided for each client if more than one treatment area is being used at a time, as in a busy salon.

Treatment Rooms

The area of the salon will help decide how many treatment rooms or cubicles one will have, and this in turn will determine how many pieces of equipment one will need. Individual treatment rooms with doors are preferable to curtained areas, since they cut down considerably on noise. However, they must not be too small or they will give a feeling of claustrophobia. There should be enough room to walk all round a couch and to manoeuvre equipment safely. Lighting should be subdued and arranged so that it does not shine in the client's eyes.

Staff Room

There should be an area where staff can sit, and where they can keep their coats and bags. There should also be a sink where they can wash their hands and clean bowls and small instruments, a steriliser for all instruments and equipment used in treatments, stock cupboards for skin-care materials and cosmetics and cleaning cupboards containing brushes, cloths, cleaners, disinfectants and other items for keeping the salon clean and tidy.

CHOOSING EQUIPMENT

Couch

Each treatment room will need a firm couch or reclining chair which can be made of wood or metal, a chouch which is a combined couch and chair, or an electrically operated couch which is a great luxury as it can be raised or lowered to suit each treatment and every aestheticienne. The couch should be comfortably upholstered with a material that can be easily wiped but without folds where oil or dust can accumulate.

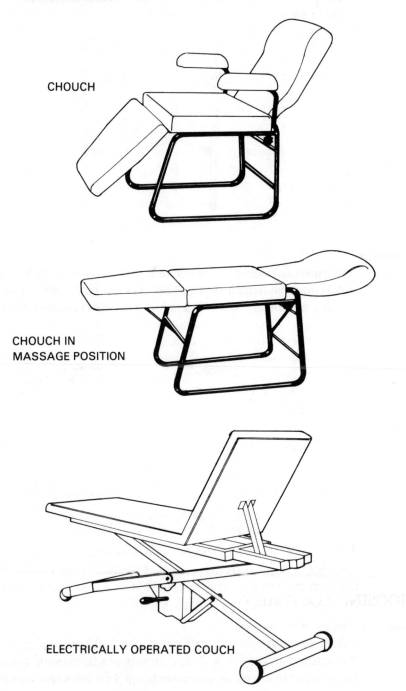

CHOUCH

CHOUCH IN
MASSAGE POSITION

ELECTRICALLY OPERATED COUCH

Trolley

A trolley is also a necessary requirement. They are available in a number of sizes, with two or three shelves. They can be of metal, wood, plastic or glass, all easily cleaned although glass can be more easily broken.

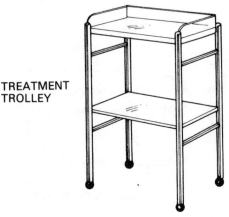

TREATMENT
TROLLEY

Steriliser

A steriliser is essential. It is not sufficient just to cleanse instruments and to store them in antiseptic. This does not kill bacteria. There are a number of different kinds to choose from: ultraviolet sterilisers will

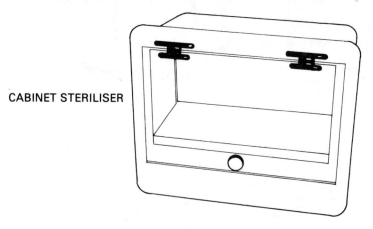

CABINET STERILISER

destroy most bacteria; steam cabinets using a fumigant such as formalin are not as expensive as other methods; steam under pressure using an autoclave is very effective, but autoclaves are expensive and are more often used in the medical field.

Other Essential Equipment

Other essential equipment includes a cold magnifier for skin examination and electrolysis and an infrared lamp (with some lamps the infrared bulb can be easily exchanged for an ultraviolet bulb), a thermo-mask or facial iron for warming the skin. A number of salons will also require a facial steamer. A high frequency unit with several different electrodes can be purchased as a salon model or in a small case. A wax heater will often be in use. If hot wax is to be used, a double wax heater will be required. For warm wax, a smaller heater is used. Electrolysis is a treatment often requested and there are a number of reliable machines available.

For the specialised treatments, a galvanic machine with facial electrodes, a vacuum suction machine with facial electrodes, a faradic machine with rollers and a heater for paraffin wax will be needed. By looking at different purveyors' establishments, one can see machines from the small to the extravagant in size as well as price.

Basic Materials

In addition stocks of the following will be needed:

towels or blankets to cover the couch and client;

gowns and headbands for the client to use;

assorted bowls and receivers;

paper couch roll to place on the couch;

tissues;

cotton-wool;

skin-care preparations and make-up for use and sale;

manicure and pedicare items;

instruments for facial treatments.

Skin-care Products and Cosmetics

There is a very wide range of skin-care and cosmetic products. One should endeavour to purchase the products required for a specific job, not necessarily the most showy or expensive. A number of the larger cosmetic houses require minimum orders which can often be very costly. Some of the smaller manufacturers are willing to sell individual items.

Whether one keeps stock for retail or merely for salon use, one must make sure that the older stock is used before the new. The simplest way to do this is to place the old stock at the front of the shelf and put the new behind it.

All skin-care and cosmetic products should be kept in a cool, dry, dark area. This will help stop them deteriorating and the labels or cartons from fading.

It is better to buy small stocks of products frequently and sell them fast than to purchase large quantities and have to keep them, in good condition, for a long time. It is a good idea to make a note of when and how much of each product was purchased.

The ideal time to sell a product is when you are using it on a client. If she likes what you are using, suggest that she might benefit from its use at home. If you give a good treatment and a woman enjoys herself, she will very often buy the products that you suggest. One must, however, be careful not to oversell or she may feel that she is being pressurised into buying too much. If one introduces just one or two products occasionally, a client will much more readily purchase them.

HOME VISITING PRACTICE

The aestheticienne who is going to have a home visiting practice will require different equipment. The main requirement is a car to transport the aestheticienne and equipment to the clients. A portable couch will help to create the impression that here is a professional ready to work. Some people try to work without a couch but it is not nearly as easy to create the same sense of professionalism.

One should take the equipment for the treatment one is to perform. For facial work an inspection lamp or magnifier is required. A small infrared lamp, thermo-mask or iron to warm the skin, or a high frequency machine may be needed. If one is going to perform electrolysis, a portable machine is available. For depilatory waxing, a warm wax kit is the easiest to transport. One should have a steriliser at home to use after cleaning all the instruments used. One also requires a case or bag containing towels, loose paper towels, tissues, cut cotton-wool, assorted bowls, lotions, creams and make-up required for the treatments, manicure, pedicare and facial instruments as needed.

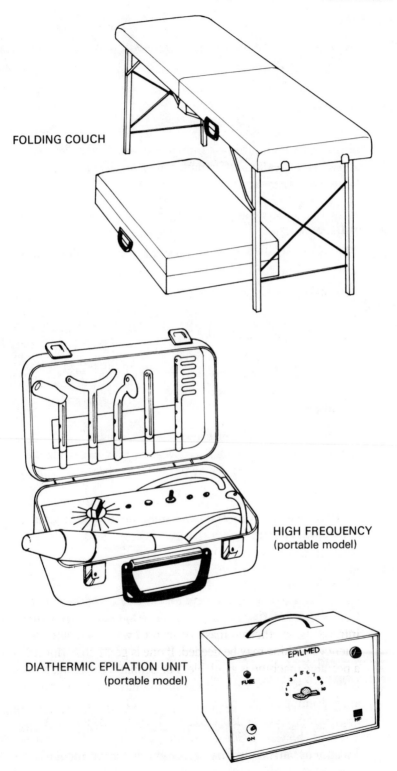

FOLDING COUCH

HIGH FREQUENCY
(portable model)

DIATHERMIC EPILATION UNIT
(portable model)

FIRST AID

Very occasionally the aestheticienne will have cause to deal with an accident or illness.

Serious conditions

For a serious condition, unless the aestheticienne is a trained first aid or medical person, the best thing she can do is to cover the patient with a blanket and call for an ambulance or medical assistance. One can so easily administer the wrong treatment.

Minor conditions

There are, however, a number of minor conditions where the aestheticienne can assist.

Fainting

This is caused by a sudden interruption of the blood flow to the brain. Prior to actually fainting the patient may have several symptoms. She may appear pale, feel weak or dizzy. Some may produce cold beads of perspiration. Others may feel an uncomfortable sensation in the abdomen. These symptoms may be followed by a short period of unconsciousness.

The patient should be placed on the floor or a couch and, if possible, the feet raised. She should be covered with a warm blanket. Smelling salts (spirits of ammonia) may be held near the nostrils and will help to stimulate her.

When she has recovered consciousness she should be given a hot drink and allowed to rest.

Burns

Burns can be classified as in three degrees.

First degree burns are when superficial damage is limited to the outer layer of the epidermis. It produces redness, heat and pain.

Second degree burns are when there is damage to the dermis and the formation of blisters.

Third degree burns are when the epidermis, dermis and underlying tissue are destroyed, producing a charred or coagulated area.

Treatment varies with the degree and extent of the burn.

For any severe burn, immediate medical attention is required. While you are awaiting help, if possible lie the patient down and keep her as still as possible. Do not attempt to remove any clothing from the area. Cover the area with a light dressing or freshly laundered handkerchief and keep the patient warm to minimise the effect of shock.

For minor burns, immerse the burnt area in cold water or wrap it in linen soaked in cold water. This serves to exclude air from the area as well as constricting the blood vessels in the area, so lessening the pain. When the initial pain has ceased, a burn dressing may be applied, although most minor burns will subside very well if exposed to the air.

Bruises

These are the result of subcutaneous bleeding usually caused by a knock. Immediate treatment is by the application of an ice pack or a quick-evaporating skin tonic. Heat may be applied after 24 hours. Severe bruising with pain may be an indication of a fracture and medical attention should be sought.

Bleeding

This is the result of a cut blood vessel. For a minor cut a firm dressing should suffice. If severe, a pressure bandage should be placed over the area and medical attention sought.

First Aid Box

All salons and clinics must keep a fully stocked first aid box.

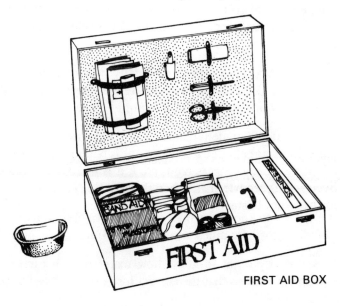

FIRST AID BOX

It should contain:

1 Antiseptic lotion
2 Burn jelly
3 Cotton-wool
4 Assorted cotton bandages
5 Crêpe bandages
6 Gauze 薄沙, 沙布
7 Small elastic plasters
8 Antacid
9 Smelling salts
10 Aspirin or similar compound
11 Small bowls
12 Scissors

ELECTRICITY

An aestheticienne should have a simple understanding of how electricity works and how to deal with minor faults.

How Electricity Works

Electricity is a form of energy which, when in motion, causes a thermal or magnetic effect, or when used in conjunction with other elements can cause a chemical or mechanical effect.

Mains electricity is usually produced by a generator at a power station on the national grid. Other generators are quite small, producing only enough electricity for a single house. Direct electricity can be stored in a battery.

There are three basic units in electricity. *Volts* can be thought of as the force of the electricity, *amps* indicate the rate at which the electricity flows, and *watts* indicate the amount of power.

In the United Kingdom mains electricity is usually at 240 volts. It is different in other countries. When one is buying equipment it is wise to check the voltage that is required. If it is not correct, the unit can be damaged. A transformer may overcome this problem.

It is helpful to know how many watts a piece of equipment uses, so you can work out how much it will cost to run.

It is also important to know how many amps a particular piece of equipment uses so that the correct fuse can be placed in the plug.

Fuses

Everyone using electricity should know how to change a fuse. A fuse is a piece of wire of a known resistance which acts as a safety device to prevent the overloading of the wire and subsequent damage of the equipment. There are two kinds of fuse, the cartridge which is fitted in to plugs and modern equipment, and the wire fuse which is extensively used for the mains fuses.

Cartridge Fuse

It is important that a cartridge fuse of the *correct amperage* is put into a plug if a fuse is required. All *modern* 13 amp plugs require one. Do not use a higher amperage fuse than is required for that piece of equipment.

Wire Fuse

Before attempting to look at a mains fuse you must switch off all the electricity at the mains. It is a good idea to have the fuse holders marked with which circuit they supply. It is also useful to have a few spare fuse holders already wired with the correct wire – 5, 10 or 15 amps.

Wiring up a Plug

When wiring up a plug, you should make sure that the correct coloured wire is connected to the corresponding pin:

brown (or red) to the *live* pin.

blue (or black) to the *negative* pin.

green/yellow (or green) to the *earth* pin.

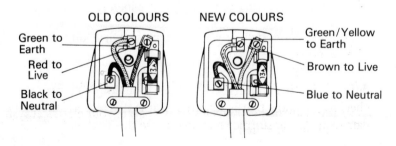

WIRING PLUGS

OLD COLOURS   NEW COLOURS

Green to Earth
Red to Live
Black to Neutral

Green/Yellow to Earth
Brown to Live
Blue to Neutral

Remember: green/yellow wire to Earth terminal (marked E or ⏚); blue wire to Neutral terminal (marked N); brown wire to Live terminal (marked L).

The screws should be firmly tightened so that the wire cannot be pulled out.

Faulty Equipment

If you find that a piece of electrical equipment does not function, switch it off at the wall, pull out the plug and check the wiring in the plug. Then check the fuse. Do *not* attempt to repair equipment while it is still plugged in.

Most equipment manufacturers will rescind any guarantee if it has been touched by any engineer other than their own, therefore you should obtain from the manufacturers the names and addresses of their approved service and repair agents.

How to Avoid Damage to Equipment

(1) Make sure that all equipment is kept clean and free of dust as this is one of the main causes of breakdown.

(2) Don't let any fluid or oil seep into the equipment.

(3) Avoid trailing wires as they can be a hazard:
(a) you can trip over them;
(b) trolleys will not run over them;
(c) they may become tangled and pull on the plug.

(4) Never remove a plug by pulling the wire. Always switch off at the socket and then carefully remove the plug holding the plug itself.

(5) Plugs should not be left plugged in to their sockets at the end of the day.

(6) If you are going to use an adaptor, make sure that you do not have too much equipment plugged in to it, causing overloading.

(7) Check the wiring of your plugs frequently.

(8) Make sure that any equipment you use directly on a client is properly earthed.

(9) Do buy your equipment from a reputable source.

(10) If you are in any doubt about any part of your electrical system, do call in a qualified electrician.

Chapter 22

The Aestheticienne

First impressions count. When the client first meets the aestheticienne, it is her appearance and attitude which will determine how well the treatment goes.

PERSONAL STANDARDS AND HYGIENE

The aestheticienne should have a pleasant and cheerful manner. She should know when to chatter and when to keep quiet so that the client can relax. It helps to have an interest in several subjects so that her conversation will consist of more than just comments on the weather.

The aestheticienne's appearance must be clean and tidy. At all times she should wear some form of overall. It need not necessarily be white. A pale pastel colour can look very smart without being too clinical. A touch of informality may help to relax a nervous or shy client. Whatever the colour, the overall should be well laundered. Any tears must be mended and lost buttons replaced.

If the aestheticienne is entitled to wear a badge from a professional organisation, she should wear it with pride. She should not wear a lot of jewellery – dangling earrings, chains, bracelets, rings or fancy watches – as they may 'catch' on the client, jangle and look unprofessional.

WEAR YOUR BADGE WITH PRIDE AND BE A CREDIT
TO YOUR SCHOOL AND ASSOCIATION

Her hair must be clean and kept off her face. If hair is allowed to fall about, it will look untidy, get in her eyes, and she will continually fidget with it. A hairband or slide will help to keep it tidy.

skin clean.

6 The skin must be seen to be clear, blemishes dealt with and stale make-up removed. If make-up is worn, it must be carefully and discretely applied.

not too sophisti-cated

6 Clients can be frightened off if they feel an aestheticienne is too sophisticated. They fear she may be unapproachable and they may hesitate to ask the very question that is worrying them.

keep teeth clean

7 Oral hygiene is very important. A regular visit to a dentist is advised and the frequent use of toothpaste and mouthwash is most important. If one enjoys hot spicy foods, an oral deodorant should be used.

use soap to keep fresh.

8 It is essential to be particular about one's personal hygiene. The judicious use of soap and water and a deodorant will help to keep you fresh.

A light perfume cologne

9 If you wish to wear a perfume, it should not be overpowering. A light perfume cologne would be sufficient.

hands are well manicured, keep nails short

10 The hands must be well manicured and the nails kept short. If they are not, it is impossible to perform many treatments effectively. A nail digging into the skin during a facial treatment or massage is not a pleasant experience, nor is the rasp of rough skin. If nail enamel is worn it must not be smudged or chipped. Hands must be washed before and after every treatment and during it if necessary.

comfortable shoes, clean & good repair. chapped

11 As an aestheticienne is on her feet most of the day, it is essential that she should wear comfortable shoes, which must be kept clean and in good repair.

The above points of personal standards and hygiene should be adhered to at all times. It is only a courtesy to one's clients to present a personal freshness to them. If an aestheticienne is untidy or lazy about her personal appearance, she is likely to be untidy or lazy in her work.

ATTITUDE TO CLIENTS

An aestheticienne must always maintain a professional attitude towards her clients.

1 The client who is being treated is deserving of your undivided attention. Put thoughts of your previous client out of your mind and do not start to think of the next client until you have finished with the present one.

2 Do not discuss one client's condition with another. Anyone who gossips will soon lose her clientele.

Be prepared to listen sympathetically to a client but do not become involved in her problems.

When a client consults you about a treatment, do not let her dictate which treatment she should have, nor how it should be carried out. *You* are the expert and if a certain treatment is right for Mrs X it may not be required by Mrs Y. However, you must take into account the client's wishes.

Keep your problems to yourself. Clients may want to unburden their problems on to you but will not particularly wish to hear yours. The old Victorian adage of avoiding the topics of sex, politics and religion still makes sense. This way one avoids disagreement with a client.

PROFESSIONAL ETHICS

An aestheticienne's conduct of her relationship with others in the same field as well as with members of other professional bodies is of great importance. Aestheticiennes should respect one another. If you cannot find anything good to say about another professional's work, it is better not to say anything. Because one aestheticienne has been trained in a different way from oneself, it does not mean to say that either way is wrong. Instead of disagreeing, it is much better to get together and exchange ideas – this way, both benefit.

When aestheticiennes work together in a salon they must present a united professional front to the clients. They must agree to carry out the same treatments and not to alter them without consulting the person responsible for the salon.

An aestheticienne should not accept any clients for a treatment who are currently receiving the same treatment elsewhere, unless they have the permission of the other aestheticienne. In other words – do not poach.

When an aestheticienne leaves a salon she should not entice clients away from her former employer, nor should she go into business in the near neighbourhood.

The aestheticienne should strive to have a good understanding with others in the 'beauty' world.

If an aestheticienne can gain the confidence of the local doctors, they are quite likely to recommend her to their patients. If a doctor does send a patient to her for a specific treatment, she must carry out that treatment in the prescribed manner. On the other hand, she must never attempt to treat a medical condition, but must refer the client to a doctor.

By the same token, an aestheticienne may perform a pedicare, but any advanced foot treatment should be referred to a chiropodist. We do well not to tread on their toes!

When you accept a person as a client you must give her your full attention and the best treatment of which you are capable.

One should be prepared to accept a person as a client regardless of colour, creed or personal circumstance.

Conclusion

When you have completed your training and leave your school or college, you may find that life is not as easy as you anticipated. Salons may not come up to the standards that you had expected. If you are working on your own, there may be a shortage of clients. Whatever happens, do not lower your own standards.

Whenever you can, seek to improve your knowledge in all aspects of your work. So much is happening in this profession that one should be continually adding to one's original knowledge, studying new techniques to see if they will work for you, discarding those that do not.

Be proud of your profession. May you have great success in it.

General Glossary

Aestheti-cienne A person who is trained to assist people to look better and feel the benefit of her skills. The treatments are usually confined to the face, décolleté, hands and feet and include facial massage, manicure, depilatory waxing, electrolysis

Actinic Relating to the active rays of the light spectrum

Acute Severe symptoms having a short duration

Adipose tissue Fatty tissue

Affinity Elements or atoms that have an attraction for each other

Albinism An absence of pigment

Alkaline A compound that has the ability to neutralise acid. It has a pH of more than 7

Allergy A sensitivity to certain substances causing an unpleasant reaction

Alopecia Baldness

Amino acids Molecules of organic acid which combine to form chains or protein

Analysis A process by which chemical substances are examined

Antibody Protein substances developed by the body in response to an invasion of foreign bodies to provide an immunity to diseases

Antidote A substance given to counteract the action of a poison

Anti-perspirant A liquid or powder applied to the skin to stop the flow of perspiration by sealing the skin

Antiseptic A substance that helps to prevent the growth of bacteria

Aqueous Pertaining to water

Aroma-therapy	A massage or treatment using essential oils of known therapeutic value and dosage
Aromatic	Having a perfume
Bacteria	A single-cell plant-like micro-organism
Biology	The study of animal or vegetable life
To contract	To reduce in size or to shorten
Cyst	A closed sac containing fluid or solid matter
Dandruff	Dry, white scales sometimes found on the scalp
Deodorant	A substance which destroys or neutralises unpleasant odours
Detergent	A synthetic soap or cleanser
Diagnosis	The recognition of a disease or condition from its symptoms
Emollient	A lotion or cream which softens the skin
Emulsion	A mixture of two liquids which would not normally mix. They are shaken together until the fat globules are broken down and thoroughly mixed together with the liquid
Exfoliation	The removal of dead scales from the skin
Fever	A rise in the body temperature above normal
Herpes simplex	A cluster of blisters often found around the mouth, commonly called 'cold sores'
Herpes zoster	An acute infection with inflammation following the path of the underlying nerve
Ingrown hair	Hair that grows under the skin
Ingrown nail	Nail that grows into the surrounding tissue
Keratoma	A thickened pad of epidermis
Lentigo	A freckle
Litmus paper	A specially treated paper which is turned red by acids and blue by alkalis

Membrane A thin layer of tissue which covers an organ or structure, separating one part from another

Mole A discoloured area raised above the surface of the skin

Naevus A congenital discoloured skin blemish

Neutral Having a pH of 7 – neither acid nor alkaline

Optic Pertaining to the eye

Ozone A form of oxygen caused by a discharge of electricity through oxygen

pH (potential of hydrogen) The pH scale expresses the degree of acidity
acid: 0–6
neutral: 7
alkaline: 8–14

Physiatrist A person trained in certain aspects of physical therapy so as to assist people to become fitter and healthier

Physical therapy Treatment of a disorder by physical means – massage, heat, electrical apparatus, etc. by a physical therapist

Physio-therapist A person trained to treat injuries, deformities and disease by massage, heat, exercises, etc.

Protein A complete organic substance found in all living matter

Psychology The study of the structure of the mind and its functions

Reflex An involuntary nerve action

Sty An inflammation of a sebaceous gland of the eyelid

Symptom Evidence of a disease or physical disability

Theory The basis on which a fact is built

Therapy Treatment of a disease or disorder

Tumor An abnormal swelling, may be benign (harmless) or malignant (carcinogenic)

Vitamins Organic substances found in most foods in minute amounts. They are essential for the maintenance of health and act as metabolic regulators

Useful Addresses

Examining Bodies

British Association of Beauty Therapy and Cosmetology
Suite 5, Wolseley House, Oriel Road, Cheltenham, Glos.

British Association of Electrolysists
6 Quakers Mede, Haddenham, Bucks. HP17 8EB

International Therapy Examination Council (I.T.E.C.)
16 Avenue Place, Harrogate, N. Yorkshire HG2 7PJ

National Federation of Health and Beauty Therapists
P.O. Box 36, Arundel, West Sussex BN18 0SW

The City and Guilds of London Institute
46 Britannia Street, London WC1 9RE

The Institute of Electrolysis
251 Seymour Grove, Manchester M16 0DS

Professional Organisations

Professional organisations offering their members services which
include public indemnity insurance:

British Association of Beauty Therapy and Cosmetology
Suite 5, Wolseley House, Oriel Road, Cheltenham, Glos.

Independent Professional Therapists' International
London Road, Retford, Notts., England.

Equipment Suppliers

Ellisons Ltd.
Crondal Road, Exhall, Coventry CV7 9NH
Tel: 0203 361619

George Solly Organisation Ltd.
James House, 50 Queen Street, Henley-on-Thames, Oxon RG9 1DF,
England.
Tel: 0491 577928

Hospital Equipment and Laboratory Products Ltd.
2b/3b North Way, Bounds Green Industrial Estate, Bounds Green,
New Southgate, London N11 2UN, England.
Tel: 01 361 9984

Ronald Hagman Ltd.
Wendover House, Beaconsfield Road, Friern Barnet, London
N11 3AB England.

Taylor Reeson Laboratories Ltd.
Carlton House, Commerce Way, Lancing, Sussex
Tel: 0903 761100

Preparations

Hand-made skin-care preparations in retail and salon sizes, Beauty Therapy products including over 30 Essential Oils blended for aromatherapy, also formulations and manufacturing of 'Own Salon Label' products may be obtained from:
Ronald Hagman Ltd.
Wendover House, Beaconsfield Road, Friern Barnet, London
N11 3AB England
Tel: 01 368 3674

Individually blended Essential Oils and full range of Aromatherapy creams and masks from:
Arnould-Taylor Para-Medical Products,
James House, Oakelbrook Mill, Newent, Glos GL18 1HD, England.
Tel: 0531 821875

Schools Association

The Association of Independent Beauty Schools Ltd.,
c/o John Cragg, Storecroft House, London Road, Retford, Notts., England.

Index